Ally Parenting:

A Non-Adversarial Approach to Transform Conflict Into Cooperation

Cynthia Klein

Editing by Kimberly Stinson Serrano and Jenna Teague.
Illustrations by Ray Cabarga and Erik Ramirez.
Author's photo by Cheryl Shepard Photography.
Cover photo by Wong Yu Liang.

Klein, Cynthia
Ally Parenting: A Non-Adversarial Approach
to Transform Conflict Into Cooperation

1. Parenting 2. Child Rearing 3. Self-Help

ISBN 978-0-9984412-1-4 Soft cover
ISBN 978-0-9984412-2-1 EBook

Library of Congress Control Number: 2017902718

This book is not intended as a substitute for
advice from a trained professional.

Published in the United States by Bridges 2 Understanding,
bridges2understanding.com

Table of Contents

Section 5 211
The Collaborator and Supporter Roles – Solving Problems

Introduction to Ally Parenting

Do you have a child who ignores you when you give directions, or argues with you like an attorney trying to change your mind, or refuses to talk to you other than with a few words or grunts? Do you sometimes feel that you and your children are more like adversaries than allies? If you do, then *Ally Parenting: A Non-Adversarial Approach to Transform Conflict Into Cooperation* is for you. Each of these challenges creates a painful wall between you and your child that can melt away with an Ally Parenting approach.

This *Ally Parenting* book is the synthesis of twenty-two years of teaching parents through private consultations, classes, and speaking engagements. Each chapter is an answer to questions parents have asked about how to get more cooperation from their children, or how to make them more responsible, or how to get their child to talk to them more. Parents came to me after trying many common strategies such as taking things away, isolating, yelling, pleading, threatening, shaming, questioning, and commanding, and they just couldn't stand it anymore.

These common authoritarian strategies create an adversarial relationship in the family. Therefore, parents are unable to influence their children and often feel like powerless victims.

They want their children to view them as an ally who will listen and discuss problems with them. At the same time, they want to be respected as the final authority in the family. The parents in this book weren't ready to give up on their families, so they reached out to me to find an alternate parenting approach that would work with their children.

As I worked with these parents, I was also raising a daughter with a strong-willed mind. I realized early on that an authoritarian, controlling parenting approach didn't work with my daughter, either. I read about one strategy on how to get kids to bring over their dishes to the sink after mealtime. The strategy taught that each time she forgot to take them over, I would take the dishes over instead and she would have to pay me as if I was her maid. When I told my daughter what we were going to do, she burst into tears and said, "I'm never going to have any money." She knew she would constantly forget.

This threat wasn't going to work because to her it was a punishment which would only leave her feeling discouraged. So, we never implemented it. Instead, we used more respectful strategies referred to in this book such as short reminders, "Your dish," or the After-Then Strategy, e.g., "After you bring over your dish, then you can watch TV." These Ally Parenting approaches were much more effective in getting the dishes to the kitchen!

As parents and I worked together, it became clear that they needed to know exactly what to say word for word. Since they didn't experience respectful parenting as children, they didn't have a reservoir of words to use. They needed to know what current words and actions were building the walls so they could stop using them. Parents also needed to know not only what to say, but how to listen so they could emotionally connect with their children. Without connection, advice on how to direct their children or do problem solving together would be ineffective. Parents who had already tried controlling their children, with damaging results, were ready to learn how to guide their children based on an emotional connection first. As a result, *Ally Parenting* was born.

In contrast to adversarial parenting, parents need to focus on how to communicate so that walls melt and bridges between parents and children are built. Because parents and I collaborated to find solutions, I consider each parent a co-author of this book. Their questions brought forth my inner wisdom based on knowledge, experience, and intuition of how we interact with one another. Then, they took my suggestions, tweaked them to fit their family, and reported back the successes and continual challenges they experienced. Thank you to the hundreds of parents requesting solutions on how to melt the walls. Your searching has been the great impetus for creating this transformation guide so you can become the parent you want to be.

My parenting philosophy is strongly influenced by Michael Popkin, PhD, who created Active Parenting. I was fortunate to begin my career as a parenting educator teaching a 6-week Active Parenting class and seeing the positive results parents were experiencing.

Dr. Popkin has graciously given me permission to build upon several of his parenting concepts in my work and in this book. The following concepts – problem ownership, goals of behavior, the Think-Feel-Do Cycle, communication blocks, responding to feelings with empathy, problem solving, and family meetings – are used with permission of the publisher, copyright © Active Parenting Publishers. His in-depth understanding about the change process resonated with me and continues to be the foundation for Ally Parenting. You will find references to Dr. Popkin's concepts throughout this book. I invite you to contact his website, www.ActiveParenting.com.

I was also privileged to assist Patty Wipfler, founder of Hand in Hand parenting, in developing her Parenting by Connection education program. She is a master at understanding how to listen deeply to children as a means to create connection and give children positive power during playtime with parents. Both concepts are integral parts of my work with parents and my own family. Thank you, Patty, for your dedication to creating happier families and for your book *Listen: Five Simple Tools to Meet Your Everyday Parenting Challenges*.

My goal is to build a more peaceful world through each family learning how to communicate respectfully and cooperatively, regardless of the parents' childhood experiences and role models. As parents, we can change the next generation and create a happier world.

The following is a story of how a mom used the tools in *Ally Parenting: A Non-Adversarial Approach to Transform Conflict Into Cooperation* to build greater harmony with her daughter.

Mom Wins Cooperation Through Soft Power

I started working with Cynthia because I wanted to reduce the conflict in my home with my two teenagers. I knew I needed to change how I approached situations and the way I was giving instructions or making "suggestions." I was suffering and I didn't know what I was doing wrong, but whatever it was wasn't working.

We worked on my beliefs and attitudes. What I thought was a normal way to interact, I came to realize, was sarcastic and hurtful. I was trying to "force" my kids to change by making them feel bad. It was hard realizing this, but as a result I changed.

Here is an example of my change. My daughter was going to church with me. When I saw what she was wearing, I knew it was not appropriate for church. In the past I would have said things like, "What are you thinking wearing that?" or "Are you kidding? You look too skanky. You're not going looking like that." This would be considered hard power which is being forceful to try and get what I want. This approach led her to being angry with me and we would end up in a fight.

Instead, I thought about the impact of my words and I tried a gentler approach, a soft power connecting approach where I would have greater influence and not get resistance. I was amazed at the results!

Instead I said, "Your outfit is cute. I think, though, that it would be good to change your boots to shoes for church." Her response was "Okay, Mom!" and off she went and happily changed. No argument at all. I'm determined to keep watching my words and win my kids' cooperation through offering suggestions in a manner that isn't a putdown. Thank you, Cynthia for your insightful suggestions!

— Mom of two teenagers

I feel confident that you can make these suggested changes work for you because I and hundreds of other parents have as well. I was motivated to change by a deep desire to create a close relationship with my teenage daughter. What is your motivation to change?

The stories throughout this book are true and the dialogue examples illustrate parenting strategies that have been successfully tried with children ages five to twenty-five, adjusting them to fit the child's age.

Thank you for joining me on your journey to creating greater harmony in your home. When you feel a wall, just know that you can melt the wall like every other parent I've worked with. You will feel wonderful when you learn how to guide and support your children in a respectful and connected way as their ally.

I look forward to having you contact me and share your stories about how Ally Parenting has created greater connection, cooperation, and harmony in your home.

—Cynthia Klein

www.allyparenting.com

How to Use This Book: A Quick-Start Approach

*A*lly Parenting: A Non-Adversarial Approach to Transform *Conflict Into Cooperation* is a step-by-step guide on how to approach each parenting challenge, understand why it happened, and learn new Ally approaches for quick results. This book is for parents who want to delve into solutions beginning with the first chapter!

The solutions I offer are my opinion based on the positive results that many, not all, of my clients have experienced. Every family is unique. Use my ideas to stimulate thinking about your own family in a new way so you can bring out your inner wisdom to find appropriate solutions. Since the ideas are general in nature, they should NOT be used as a substitute for getting qualified professional psychological, medical, or legal help should the need arise. If you read a suggestion and you think, *I couldn't say that,* or *That wouldn't work with my child,* then think of words that would work. My goal is for the Ally Parenting approach to inspire you to change yourself first, because this is the quickest way to create a positive change in your family.

Ally Parenting helps you transform your current parenting challenges by teaching you how to choose and then apply appropriate solutions. In order to get the most out of this book, I have laid out a clear process for you to follow. Be sure to read the material entitled, *The Step-by-Step Solutions Guide.* It is the key to your success. Make copies of this guide to use for each challenge you face. Reading through this process before delving into the book will give you a clear understanding of how the information you read fits into the bigger picture of how to transform your family.

Ally Parenting is divided into five sections. Each section focuses on a different area of change that, when practiced, will bring about a positive change in your child. It's important to begin by reading and practicing the guidance in Sections 1 and 2, The Ally Parenting Approach and Creating Open Communication.

These two sections teach the foundational concepts for the entire book, so don't skip them.

Here is a summary of what you will learn in each section.

Section 1
The Ally Parenting Approach – Your Parenting Role

With this section, you begin the mental shift from adversarial thinking to Ally thinking. In Chapter 8, *Choose Your Parental Role: Director, Collaborator, or Supporter,* you will learn the essential step of how to choose your parenting role, which will determine what section of the book you will study to learn the appropriate solutions.

Section 2
Creating Open Communication

Now that your mind is open to the value of connection, you will learn what words you've been using that hurt your child. Then, the excitement happens when you stop blocking communication, practice listening with empathy, and watch your child open up as a beautiful connection transpires.

Section 3
Understanding Yourself and Your Child

This section delves into the thoughts behind adversarial parenting and the new Ally thoughts that need to replace them to make your parenting changes stick. Your power lies in knowing that change begins with you. Then, when you understand the goals behind your child's negative behavior, you can stop blaming them and instead guide them in a positive direction.

Sections 4 and 5 teach you specific strategies for the three parenting roles of Director, Collaborator, and Supporter. Change takes time, so it's important not to feel overwhelmed and try to change every problem at once. Even one or two key changes can quickly improve the harmony in your home. Pick the parenting role you want to focus on first and one or two strategies to try.

Section 4
The Director Role – Setting Limits and Boundaries

This section will teach you how to give directions that aren't ignored – while avoiding a power struggle. Begin by reading Chapter 20, *Choose the Discipline Path for Family Harmony,* and Chapter 23, *Director Parenting Role: The After-Then Strategy,* then select whichever chapters relate to your specific challenge.

Section 5
The Collaborator and Supporter Roles – Solving Problems Together

When you practice problem solving together, as a Collaborator, or support your child's problem-solving process, as a Supporter, you will be utilizing all the skills in sections one through three. Therefore, it's important to practice these skills before attempting the Collaborator or Supporter Parenting Roles.

Take your change process slowly because change takes time and it's important not to feel overwhelmed. You will be amazed how one small change by you can create big changes in your family. It's important to clearly understand your challenge and what parenting role to use so you will choose the correct small change. So, start with Section 1 and watch your perspective of your children and your parenting role shift from adversarial beliefs and actions to Ally beliefs and actions.

The Step-by-Step Solutions Guide

This action process is a step-by-step guide about how to think about your current challenges, evaluate them accurately, and then find an effective solution to try using my book, *Ally Parenting: A Non-Adversarial Approach to Transform Conflict Into Cooperation*. The questions below reflect the process I use when I'm evaluating a parent's situation and giving advice. I encourage you to make copies of this process for your personal use so you can reuse it for each challenge you encounter. Complete the seven steps to reveal your contributions to the problem so you can make specific changes that will transform your conflicts into cooperation.

Don't give up if the situation seems to get worse before getting better. Since your child is used to negative behavior patterns, it can take a while before they see the benefit of positive behavior patterns.

I suggest reading Section 1, The Ally Parenting Approach and Section 2, Creating Open Communication, before using this process.

Write down the challenge you want to solve. Be as specific as possible, such as, "My child dawdles in the morning, so we leave late." I'll use this problem as an example throughout this process sheet.

My challenge to solve is...

_____

_____

_____

_____

_____

_____

1. Determine what parenting role or roles you will use to solve this problem.

Refer to Chapter 8, *Choose Your Parental Role: Director, Collaborator, or Supporter,* found in Section 1. In the example above, you would use two roles. First, you'll act as a Collaborator to discuss and plan a solution together, and then most likely you will need to use Director strategies to ensure follow-through from your children.

The parenting role(s) I will use to solve this problem is/are: *Check those that apply to this particular challenge.*

- ❑ Director Role (parent decides)
- ❑ Collaborator Role (parent and child decide together)
- ❑ Supporter/Confidant Role (child decides)

2. Determine what goal(s) your child is trying to achieve through a negative approach.

Refer to Chapter 16, *Why Children Do What They Do - It's Not About You.*

Write down the negative behavior your child is doing next to the appropriate goal(s). For example: Belonging – My child dawdles so I have to keep reminding him, which gives him attention and a sense of belonging. Power – My child is dawdling so he can feel powerful by rebelling and not doing what I ask him to do.

1. Belonging _____

_____

2. Power _____

_____

3. Protection _____

_____

4. Withdrawal _____

_____

5. Challenge _____

_____

3. Determine your current beliefs and thoughts that are keeping you from acting effectively.

Refer to the chapters in Section 1, *Are You an Ally or an Adversary?* and *Self-Knowledge is the First Step Toward Change.* Then read *Problem Solving Together Requires Flexible Thinking,* in Section 3.

Part A:

Which of these adversarial beliefs do you have?

Adversarial Beliefs That Break Connection

a. Parents are right all the time because they are adults, and children need to learn how to obey. Whether parents and children feel connected isn't important.

b. The adult has the final word, and it doesn't matter whether the child feels misunderstood, unheard, or unloved.

c. When my child misbehaves, their behavior reflects on me and means that I'm not a good parent. (This usually leads to me feeling angry at my child for embarrassing me.)

d. I need to repeatedly point out imperfections in my children so that they can change for the better.

e. Children act badly because they're trying to get back at or manipulate their parents.

f. I know what's best for my child to become successful in the future.

g. It's helpful to get angry at children so they learn that their behavior is wrong. They learn from feeling bad about themselves. Being nice won't make them regret their behavior and change.

h. "Time out" makes children think about what they've done wrong.

i. My children need to live up to my expectations of them without questioning or disagreeing with me. I know what's best for them.

j. When children start to get out of control, I need to put more controls on them.

Are there any additional problematic beliefs that you have?

_____

_____

_____

_____

_____

_____

Part B:

When your child presents a challenge, which of these inflexible thoughts do you have? These thoughts make your child the problem and therefore disempower your ability to change yourself and thus the situation:

a. _You're doing this to annoy me._

b. _You're trying to manipulate me._

c. _If you followed my advice, you wouldn't have these problems._

d. _It's no use. I'm giving up. You're on your own._

e. _You don't care about what I think or feel._

f. _You're trying to test me._

g. *This behavior is intolerable.*

h. *You never listen.*

i. *How dare you...? (talk to me that way, etc.)*

j. *You're getting out of control.*

k. *You're so (stubborn, lazy, inconsiderate, careless, selfish, etc.)*

l. *You're deliberately being (mean, uncooperative, manipulative, rude, etc.)*

Do you have any other thoughts during the conflict that make you unable to creatively find a solution?

_____

_____

_____

_____

_____

_____

4. What new flexible thoughts could you practice having during the challenge that would enable you to take responsibility to improve the situation?

a. *Maybe I need to stop and listen closely to my child.*

b. *My child is trying to meet her needs in the best way she knows how. I can create a new, positive path instead.*

c. *I need to learn how to support my child's thinking about her problems rather than telling her what to do.*

d. *I need to stop controlling, then abandoning, and instead become an effective Supporter.*

e. *My child does care even if she isn't showing it right now. She is taking care of herself.*

f. *My child is exhibiting developmentally appropriate behavior.*

g. *My child has needs and goals and is trying to cope.*

h. *I need to get control of myself and express expectations so they are heard.*

i. *I'm taking this challenge personally and defensively. Instead, I need to learn what's behind the negative behavior.*

j. *I need to find a more effective way to build cooperation rather than trying to control my child through anger and threats.*

k. *The more I label my child, the more discouraged, uncooperative, and hurt they become.*

l. *My child wants to be cooperative and connected. His emotions are not allowing him to think clearly right now. How can I help him release his emotions so he can think better?*

5. Determine which communication blocks you're using during this challenge.

Refer to the Section 2 chapters, *Awareness of Communication Blocks Is the First Step* and *Why Kids Reject Our Help – and How to Win their Trust.*

What I say that hurts my child and blocks him/her from listening:

_____

_____

_____

_____

_____

_____

I used these communication blocks. Check those that apply.

- ❏ commanding
- ❏ giving advice
- ❏ placating
- ❏ interrogating
- ❏ distracting
- ❏ psychologizing
- ❏ sarcasm
- ❏ moralizing
- ❏ being a know-it-all
- ❏ me-tooism

6 Determine which empathetic statements you could use to connect with your child during this challenge.

You will still set the expectation if you are in the Director Role. Do not add "but" after your empathy statement. Refer to the Section 2 chapters, *The Emotional Support Process Connects You to Your Child, Empathy Improves Connection and Communication,* and *Parent Success Stories Using Empathetic Responses.*

For example, if your child is still dawdling after making a morning plan, you could say, "It looks like you are having fun now. Remember our plan. It's time to get dressed."

Which of these empathetic responses could you use? You may need to try several of them to see what words keep your child expressing herself so the tensions release and clearer thinking can follow.

a. "That sounds like a real problem."

b. "You seem (upset, bored, irritated, angry, overwhelmed, frustrated, etc.)"

c. "It looks like you'd rather do _____than _____right now."

d. "Hmm, I see. It can be hard (writing a paper, having a friend mad at you, putting your phone away, etc.)"

e. "I'm sorry to hear that."

f. "I'm here for you. You're safe with me."

g. "It's hard to know what to do."

h. "That seems challenging."

What are other empathetic statements you could use?

_____

_____

_____

_____

_____

7   Put it all together. Review your answers on the above questions and write them on the lines provided, under the appropriate heading. Use this information to determine what strategies you will try first.

My challenge is:

_____

_____

_____

_____

_____

My parenting role(s) is/are:

_____

_____

_____

_____

_____

The goal(s) my child is meeting negatively is/are:

_____

_____

_____

_____

_____

_____

Depending on this goal, I will direct my child to meet their goal positively by using a strategy that develops: Check those that apply.

- ❑ Belonging: Contributing and Cooperating
- ❑ Power: Independence
- ❑ Protection: Assertiveness and Forgiveness
- ❑ Withdrawal: Appropriate Avoidance
- ❑ Challenge: Safe Adventures

In the dawdling example, you would pick strategies that develop a feeling of contribution and independence such as problem solving together to improve the morning situation so everyone is happier.

My new flexible thoughts will be:

_____

_____

_____

_____

_____

_____

The communication blocks I will avoid are:

_____

_____

_____

_____

_____

_____

The empathy statements I could use are:

The next step is to review the above information and decide on one, or maybe two, strategies you are going to try first to fix this challenge. Go to the appropriate section, listed below, for the Director Role or the Collaborator and Supporter Roles to research possible solutions. Remember that one small change done properly can have a big positive impact.

To find and decide on Director Role strategies, review Section 4, The Director Role – Setting Limits and Boundaries.

To find and decide on Collaborator or Supporter Role strategies, review Section 5, The Collaborator and Supporter Roles – Solving Problems Effectively.

The strategy or strategies I will try first are:

_____

_____

_____

_____

_____

_____

Parents often write reminders of their new thoughts and words on cards and post them in the house or car until they have successfully replaced their old habits. Perhaps you have a friend or partner who will be making changes along with you and you can compassionately remind each other.

I will remind myself of the changes I want to make by:

_____

_____

_____

_____

_____

_____

Before making changes, share with your child the changes you plan to make. One way or another, children are blamed for the problem and their misbehavior. The parent's underlying belief is often, *If my child changed, we wouldn't have this problem.* As a result, children feel hurt, and then hurt their parents back through words such as, "I hate you," and "you're so mean," or by resisting change and cooperation. When you use the Ally Parenting approach and take responsibility for changing yourself first, your children's hearts open up, their walls come down, and positive progress can be made.

For example, regarding the dawdling child, in the evening, you could say, "I've been yelling at you in the morning, which doesn't make either of us feel good. Instead, we're going to figure out a morning plan together, because it's a challenge for all of us to solve together. Then, I'll calmly make sure everyone follows our agreement in the morning. Everyone can change."

I will share the changes I plan to make with my child this way:

_____

_____

_____

_____

_____

_____

After a few days of trying your new approach, review your results. It's difficult to change because we tend to automatically fall back into old patterns, especially under duress. My approaches are very detailed and specific. Reread them several times and assess honestly what you are thinking, saying, and doing.

My experience has been that sometimes parents put great effort into changing and they still may not get the desired results. Here are a few reasons why your approach might not be working:

a. You haven't been specific enough in following my structure. For example, with the After-Then Strategy, you may resort back to a threat of, "If you don't…," or forget to add an emotionally connecting comment, or repeat the After-Then Strategy two (or even three) times and then give up and give in. With challenging children who are used to getting their way, your calm persistence and confidence (even faked confidence) is essential.

b. You've chosen the wrong role. Parents often direct because they want their children to succeed, when instead they should be solving the problem together or supporting their child's thought process as a Collaborator or a Supporter.

c. You haven't changed your thinking about your child or about the challenge from an adversary to an ally, so you're inconsistent with the Ally approach. Therefore, you won't be successful. For example, if you're still blaming your child in your mind, you won't have honest empathetic thoughts, and you won't be able to connect, which is the basis of influencing your child toward change.

d. Ally Parenting provides tools that can be used for all kinds of children. At the same time, your child may need their own support from a specialist. For example, if your child has a very difficult time focusing and cooperating even after using these tools, you may seek a specialist for testing and additional professional guidance.

My approach isn't working because...

_____

_____

_____

_____

_____

_____

and I determine to...

_____

_____

_____

_____

_____

_____

Special Note from the Author: It can often feel like too much effort to change, and it's difficult to remember. It's easier to change when you have support, so ask your partner, friend, or loved one to remind you of your determination and that the pain of change is less than the pain of staying stuck. Focus on one issue at a time, because small steps can have big results. Congratulate yourself each time you catch yourself making a mistake and recommit to changing the next time. Children are usually forgiving when you apologize and let them know what you'll do differently next time. Your change teaches your children how to change. Don't give up! You are the guiding light within your family.

Section 1

The Ally Parenting Approach
- Your Parenting Role

1.
Ask the Right Questions to Find the Right Parenting Solutions

In my experience as a parenting educator and coach, parents who struggle with finding discipline solutions are often approaching their kids from a controlling perspective. They come to me because they've tried every tactic they know to make their kids comply and still haven't been successful.

They are hoping there's one more strategy they haven't learned yet that will fix the problem. They keep looking and hoping until they find me.

First off, let's review the common questions that parents ask:

"How do I control my child so he will stop hitting his brother?"

"How do I get my teen to do their homework?"

"Why is my child so lazy, selfish, uncooperative, or ungrateful?"

"Why doesn't she try harder?"

"Why is my child so difficult? Why do they always argue?"

"How do I get my child off of their phone, computer games, or video games?"

Each of these questions comes from a parent's feeling of powerlessness, fear, discouragement, confusion, judgment, misunderstanding, or hopelessness. Parents feel a lack of connection and positive influence with their children. There's a gap that they can't figure out how to bridge.

The common questions listed above are adversarial because they blame children rather than take joint ownership for the struggles parents have with them. This stance creates an "us versus them" mindset.

When children are viewed as the source of the problems, then parents must fix them in order to fix the problems. This leads to parental attempts at controlling and managing children, which often brings out rebellion and revenge in return.

Imagine a parent-child equation where the parent's thoughts and actions on one side influence the child's thoughts and actions on the other side. When your side changes, the other side changes in response. You may ask, "But what if I do what you say and they still act the same?" They won't. I have never witnessed an instance in which parents changed and their kids didn't change in return.

The true power to create greater family happiness comes from parents focusing on how they can change first. This Ally approach of standing alongside your children is the most influential and respectful way to address problems and bring about the positive changes everyone desires.

Children, like their parents, don't want strife in the family. They behave as best they can for their maturity level, so that's why it is up to us to make the changes. Recently, I was working with a mom of two teenagers. She felt stuck because she wasn't able to change her sons. She asked me adversarial questions to find controlling solutions. Instead, I explained how the parent-child equation works. She was skeptical.

At our first session, I instructed her to go home and tell her children that she's trying to make changes, show them what she's working on, and solicit their input. Two days later, I contacted her to find out her teens' response. This is what she said: "The children were very receptive to my new instructions from you and willing to see what evolves. I did get some feedback on things they'd like to see change in the home as well."

With her willingness to take responsibility for making changes and soliciting input from her children, this mom has already experienced greater cooperation and happiness in her home.

She is now learning to be an ally, walking alongside her children and working together to make everyone in the family happier.

Here are examples of Ally Parenting questions that will lead you to your true power to make positive changes between you and your children:

♥ How do I create a supportive home?

♥ How do I listen better?

♥ How do I help my child?

♥ What do I need to change about myself?

♥ How do I manage my emotions and respond with logic when making decisions?

♥ What will make our family members feel more connected to each other?

♥ What am I doing that continues this negative cycle?

♥ How can I open up to my children and have dialogue about how we can improve the family together?

♥ Can I demonstrate vulnerability and courage to my children by taking responsibility for our challenges without asking them to change as well (while knowing that they will automatically)?

Try these Ally questions and see how much more hopeful you feel that change is possible. Know that your children want a happier family, too. They are simply waiting for you to lead the way.

2.
Are You an Ally or an Adversary?

Interacting with your children can sometimes feel like walking on eggshells where any comment or action could crush the "egg" causing a gooey mess. Cleaning up after conflicts is challenging and time-consuming. To avoid the need for clean-up, I recommend learning how to interact with your children as an ally rather than an adversary. An Ally parent knows how to build greater influence than an adversary parent. Approaching family interactions as an ally will create more cooperative and peaceful relationships between family members for a lifetime.

Historically, parents have had adversarial relationships with their children. Every parent I know can easily give examples of parenting statements that put them at odds with their child. Examples of these types of statements include, "Because I said so," "I'm the parent," and "Do what you're told." Leaving behind the adversary parenting approach and learning how to become an Ally parent requires study, effort, and practice to perfect your skills.

An adversarial parenting position is defined by two main features. The first is that a disagreement ends with the parent winning and the child losing, i.e., a win-lose solution. Putting children in the powerless and demeaning position of losing is not as widely accepted now as it was in the past. The second feature of adversarial parenting is disregard for the child's feelings and thoughts during a disagreement. Since the quality of the parent-child relationship is not of primary concern, the child ends up feeling misunderstood, unheard, or unloved.

In contrast, the Ally Parenting position strives for a win-win solution to conflicts. The parent is still the final authority, yet the child doesn't feel demeaned by and inferior to the parent.

Also, the parent values the parent-child relationship and the child's emotional well-being during their interactions. Even when the child doesn't get what she wants, she still feels that her parents value her opinions and they will try to reach a win-win solution, if possible.

Let's put this theory into a real-life situation where your child asks to go to the movies and your answer is "no." You've already made plans to visit Grandma, and you don't want to change your plans.

Let's see how the adversarial parent would respond:

Child: "My friends have asked me to go to the movies with them on Saturday afternoon. Can I go?"

Parent: "No, you can't go."

Child: "Why not? I really want to go, and my friends are going. You never let me do anything." (Resentment builds up against the adversarial parent, often leading to statements of magnification and confrontation.)

Parent: "No, we're doing something else."

Child: "I want to go with my friends!!!" (This argument will continue with both parent and child digging in their heels and trying to win rather than problem solving together. In the end, no one will be happy.)

An Ally-in-training interaction might sound like this:

Child: "My friends have asked me to go to the movies with them on Saturday afternoon. Can I go?"

Parent: "No, honey, because we're visiting Grandma that day."

Child: "I'd rather go to the movies. Can't you go without me?"

Parent: "The movies sound fun, and I know your friends are important, BUT visiting your grandma is more important."

Child: "I want to see my friends instead. (This argument will likely continue with poor resolution.)"

In this example, the parent started out with an empathetic Ally statement, "The movies sound fun, and I know your friends are important," and then made a very common mistake. The parent said *but*. When a person hears the word *but*, everything that was said before is no longer felt or heard. The parent's empathizing is lost, and the child suddenly views the parent as an adversary because she hears, *visiting your grandmother is more important than your friends are.*

Here's how an accomplished Ally parent could proceed:

Child: "My friends have asked me to go to the movies with them on Saturday afternoon. Can I go?"

Parent: "I see. (pause) I had made plans for our family to visit your grandma that day. I forgot to tell you."

Child: "I really want to go to the movies. It's important."

Parent: "I wouldn't feel good cancelling our plans with Grandma. Can we talk more to see if there's a way you can do both?"

Child: "Oh, OK."

The underlying belief of the Ally parent is: *How do I keep the relationship intact and try to meet everyone's needs? My goal is to find win-win solutions whenever possible.* One of the best ways to receive respect, cooperation, and appreciation from your children is to work toward becoming an ally rather than an adversary. As an ally, you will model the importance of listening to emotions, stating clear boundaries and expectations, and cooperatively solving problems together.

3.
The Adversary to Ally Transformation Process

When parents want to transform their relationship with their child, they feel excited, hopeful, and overwhelmed, all at the same time. At the start of the process, parents have difficulty understanding the cause of the conflict with their child and why their current solutions aren't effective. They've done their best when trying to implement the strategies they've learned so far from books and classes, but still, the conflict remains. This confused and stuck beginning state is Step 1 of the Adversary to Ally Transformation Process.

Step 2 of the process begins with self-reflection about what you're thinking and how your thoughts are triggering feelings and actions during conflicts. Rather than asking the question, *How can I get my child to change?*, Step 2 of the transformation process starts with asking yourself, *What am I thinking that's causing me to act ineffectively?* This question comes from a position of power because, as an adult, the prefrontal cortex of your brain is fully developed, which gives you the capacity to reflect on your thought process.

Since a child's prefrontal cortex, or logical brain, doesn't fully mature until their mid-20s, it's up to you to change first and then influence your child through this change. Often, if you ask a child why they did something, they will respond, "I don't know," because they truly don't know. As their prefrontal cortex develops and as you have calm and loving discussions with them about their behavior, their ability to self-reflect and take responsibility for changing will increase.

It's essential to understand that you are the driver of change in your family, not your child. During Step 2 of the transformation process, you pay attention to your ineffective actions after the fact, begin to analyze what went wrong, and make determinations about what to do differently next time. The same conflict often recurs, so you have plenty of opportunities to reflect afterward and learn how to stop yourself midstream, which is where the excitement begins.

For example, you might be in the habit of talking to the back of your child's head, saying, "Get off the computer now." You may have been ignored by your child in these instances or told, "I will when I finish this game." Then, you might have quickly thought, *My child is disrespecting me. I would never have done this to my parents*, which led to you feeling hurt and expressing that hurt through anger and yelling. During Step 2 of the transformation process, you realize the thought triggers that make you lash out and cause the situation to escalate into a power struggle. As you become more aware, you begin to stop yourself midstream by using your logical brain, calming yourself down, and trying again with a more effective approach.

In Step 3 of the transformation process, you focus on changing ineffective patterns in order to proactively direct your behavior while decreasing the likelihood of responding emotionally to your environment. As compared with Step 1, in Step 3 it's no longer a mystery why your kids are being un-cooperative. You aren't looking outside yourself for a solution while thinking and doing the same things and expecting a different response. You are much more enlightened than before. Your efforts to change, which have not been easy, are paying off. Knowing what to do and stopping yourself beforehand and actually making the change are two different skill sets that you've likely been working on for several months.

By now, you've mastered a few basic strategies that work in certain situations most of the time, such as the After-Then Strategy and the It's Time Strategy. You feel excited about the positive transformation that's taking place within you and the positive results you're seeing in your child. Now, you're aware when you're about to bark an order at your child to get off the computer. You manage to stop yourself and, instead, position yourself right next to your child and say, "I can see you're having fun playing that game. It's 7:00 o'clock now, so it's time for you to stop." Wow! You don't become emotional, which feels wonderful. If your child complains, you tell yourself that's to be expected and repeat, "It's time to get off the computer. You can play more tomorrow."

In Step 4 of the transformation process, your willingness to let go of preconceived ineffective ideas and embrace new ones brings you great rewards in all areas of your life. The changes you make because you're tired of conflict and want to get along better with your child are now positively impact-ing all areas of your life, e.g., marriage, work, friendship, and extended family. Everyone marvels at your change. Your new beliefs and actions are feeling normal now, and the old you is melting away, along with all the disharmony you experienced on a daily basis with your family. If you're tired and pushed to your limit, the old you might pop up, but now you know what to do to get back into harmony with your family members.

I went through the Adversary to Ally Transformation Process with my own family in order to eradicate my tendency to feel hurt, get mad, and yell. I believed I was right and wanted to control others. I worked on analyzing why I was getting mad and what I was thinking that led to feeling ignored, unloved, and unimportant. I studied, self-reflected, and learned that when my daughter didn't do what I told her to do, it wasn't against me. Rather, she was trying to get her needs met. When my husband talked about himself when I wanted him to listen to me, it wasn't that he didn't value what I had to say. Instead, he believed that he was contributing to the conversation in a meaningful way.

Because of my changes, I brought out more positive and loving responses from my daughter and husband. The shifts I made were so significant that a good friend told me I was nicer and had changed since I had my daughter. Because I was able to change in this way, I believe that you can, too. Along with Ally Parenting strategies, all you need is determination, perseverance, and the belief that when you change, you and your family members will be happier. I encourage you to take the first step and become the master of your mind, because this is the true road to happiness.

Adversary to Ally Transformation Process

Step 1

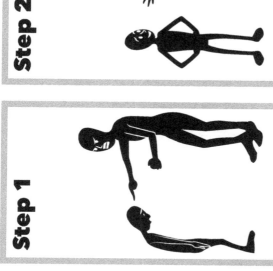

The process begins with the adult, unaware of negative thoughts, behaving adversarially and creating a wall between parent and child.

Step 2

Adult identifies the negative thoughts, then replaces with positive ones and practices Ally Parenting behavior.

Step 3

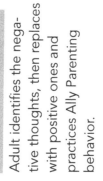

Adult, now free of negative thoughts that caused the adversarial behavior, uses newly learned Ally Parenting skills and wall between parent and child melts away.

Step 4

Adult, now skilled in Ally Parenting, has eliminated the wall between parent and child which results in a mutually loving, peaceful, and cooperative family.

4.
Self-Knowledge Is the First Step Toward Change

Knowing whether you're approaching your child as an ally or an adversary is tricky. You're reading this book because you want to be an ally. Your intention is in alignment with the Ally Parenting approach, yet you probably have some beliefs, usually learned in childhood, that make it difficult for you to act as an ally during conflict.

Our world functions in an adversarial way in all types of relationships, from nation-to-nation to parent-to-child. There is a strong tendency to use hard power and take an adversarial stance when your power and authority are threatened. I admire your willingness to look at your beliefs and scrutinize the conflict you feel when you're unable to act in the way you want. You may experience your whole being screaming to use power and control through threats, yelling, and humiliation, rather than using your inner strength and compassion to listen, be respectful, and guide.

We are able to influence our children when they feel connected to us. In other words, we can create internal change within our children through connection only, not control. Below are beliefs that form the basis of actions, either as an ally or an adversary. These beliefs are not absolute. Rather, I hope you use them as a springboard to better understand how you're thinking when it's difficult to act as an ally. Then, resolve to discard your adversarial beliefs and embrace more Ally beliefs so you can successfully implement the strategies in this book.

Ally Beliefs That Build Connection

♥ My parenting actions are based on the belief that I am emotionally and physically available for my child as much as possible. Connection comes first.

♥ The relationship between me and my child is more important than being right all the time.

♥ Listening to all of my child's emotions with love and concern, instead of disapproval and disinterest, will build a strong bond of connection between us.

♥ I believe in my children's potential and joyfully encourage them, even when their capabilities seem to be hidden or dormant at that moment.

♥ All family members are creating a home that is an oasis of support, warmth, and rejuvenation.

♥ I shouldn't expect my child to be perfect or act like an adult.

♥ Children's basic nature is to love their parents. A feeling of disconnection from others can lead to misbehavior and poor thinking. In order to help them meet their needs positively, I try to view my children's misbehavior from their perspective.

- ♥ Each adult and child brings unique strengths to the family that compensate for shortcomings in others.

- ♥ My child is his/her own person, and it is not for me to mold him/her to my own expectations. I will hold my judgment and criticism in check when they are hurtful.

- ♥ When my children get angry at me for my behavior, I will stop and take responsibility for my part, rather than denying and defending myself.

Adversarial Beliefs That Break Connection

- Parents are right all the time because they are adults, and children need to learn how to obey. Whether parents and children feel connected isn't important.

- The adult has the final word, and it doesn't matter whether the child feels misunderstood, unheard, or unloved.

- When my child misbehaves, their behavior reflects on me and means that I'm not a good parent. (This usually leads to me feeling angry at my child for embarrassing me.)

- I need to repeatedly point out imperfections in my children so that they can change for the better.

- Children act badly because they're trying to get back at or manipulate their parents.

- I know what's best for my child to become successful in the future.

- It's helpful to get angry at children so they learn that their behavior is wrong. They learn from feeling bad about themselves. Being nice won't make them regret their behavior and change.

- A "time out" makes children think about what they've done wrong.

- My children need to live up to my expectations of them without questioning or disagreeing with me. I know what's best for them.

- When children start to get out of control, I need to put more controls on them.

When parents cling to adversarial beliefs, they become rigid and averse to change. Change requires self-reflection and openness to your child's point of view and needs. If you were raised by adversarial parents, being open and vulnerable can feel weak.

In reality, adversarial parents are the weak ones, so they wield power over others. An Ally parent, by comparison, is strong, so they use influence to guide others. In this book, I will show you how and when to be strong through respect, as well as how and when to be vulnerable and respected at the same time. Take a chance, and shift toward more Ally thinking and parenting. What do you have to lose? It's time to discard the beliefs that aren't working for your family.

5.
Soft Power Creates Cooperation, Not Conflict

Imagine you are having a power struggle with your child. You're feeling angry, frustrated, and maybe even powerless because your child isn't cooperating. You might be thinking one or all of these inflexible thoughts: *You are so inconsiderate. You're defying me. You're trying to test me.* Parents often feel crazy when they're trying to move their child who has become an immovable object. To transform this craziness into calmness, begin by changing your thinking.

If your child feels that you are trying to control him, that you are not on his side, the power struggle begins. This is because each person needs power. We can fulfill our own need for power through either a soft power approach or a hard power approach with our children. When your perspective is, *How can I help my child meet their developmental needs while meeting my own simultaneously?* then you are walking alongside rather than pushing against them. As a result, your son or daughter will feel your love and support and thus be more willing to cooperate.

Aesop's fable, "The North Wind and the Sun," illustrates the hard power and soft power approaches and contrasts their effectiveness.

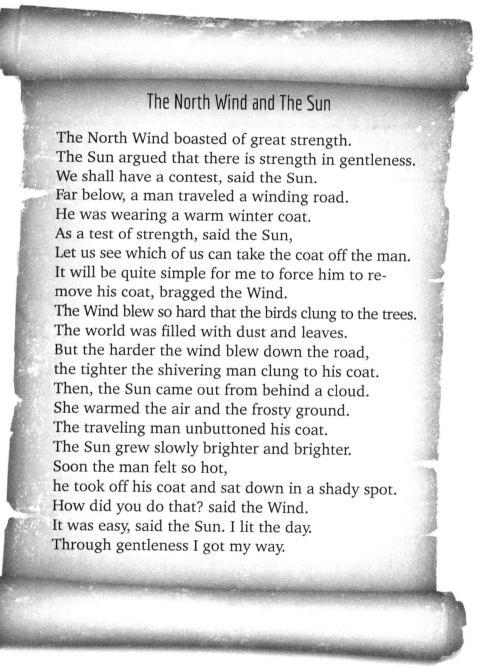

The North Wind and The Sun

The North Wind boasted of great strength.
The Sun argued that there is strength in gentleness.
We shall have a contest, said the Sun.
Far below, a man traveled a winding road.
He was wearing a warm winter coat.
As a test of strength, said the Sun,
Let us see which of us can take the coat off the man.
It will be quite simple for me to force him to re-
move his coat, bragged the Wind.
The Wind blew so hard that the birds clung to the trees.
The world was filled with dust and leaves.
But the harder the wind blew down the road,
the tighter the shivering man clung to his coat.
Then, the Sun came out from behind a cloud.
She warmed the air and the frosty ground.
The traveling man unbuttoned his coat.
The Sun grew slowly brighter and brighter.
Soon the man felt so hot,
he took off his coat and sat down in a shady spot.
How did you do that? said the Wind.
It was easy, said the Sun. I lit the day.
Through gentleness I got my way.

When a power struggle is brewing, consider this fable and choose the path of the Sun. Look for ways to build cooperation through win-win thinking. This Ally approach involves give-and-take fueled with mutual respect.

Here are some common examples of power struggle-triggering thoughts and possible cooperation-building thoughts you can use to replace them.

Power Struggle-Triggering Thoughts – The Wind	Cooperation-Building Thoughts – The Sun
You are so inconsiderate.	*This is a developmental stage. Things will change. Be patient and don't label.*
You're defying me.	*My child has needs and is trying to cope. I need to try a more effective approach.*
You're trying to test me.	*Perhaps I need to set clearer boundaries and limits.*
I can't stand it.	*I need to get control of myself.*
You never listen to me.	*I need to be more effective in my communication.*

When you choose cooperation-building thoughts, you shift the power from controlling your children as an adversary to changing yourself first. Therefore, the power struggle loses its Wind and gentleness wins.

The theory of the Think-Feel-Do Cycle explains why changing your thoughts is key to positively influencing your children.

This Cycle suggests that we often quickly respond to a power struggle conflict with strong feelings and actions triggered by our thinking about the event and the people involved. We can try to change our actions first — by not yelling at our kids, for example. This is a fantastic start. To create more permanent change, I believe we need to analyze the thinking behind our feelings and actions. If we continue to think in a power struggle-producing way while trying to act in a cooperation-building manner, our Think-Feel-Do Cycle will be incongruent, and we will not be very effective.

The more we self-reflect on our part of the power struggle and how we can change, the more we're developing our emotional intelligence. Rather than reacting emotionally and resorting to hard power, we can learn how to label and manage our emotions. This change toward our children is what it takes to be an ally who gently guides with soft power strategies like the Sun. As you change, you will also be teaching your kids how to self-reflect and learn that they have the power to change as well. Just imagine how wonderful your life will be when your children follow your lead and take responsibility to become more cooperative so that everyone can transform craziness into calmness in your family.

6.
Child Rearing: An Opportunity for Personal Growth

My own parenting philosophy focuses on emotional connection first, and this focus has enriched my life as a parent immeasurably. My work as a parent educator is based on this goal of improving family connections in order to enhance the child's well-being, potential, and success in life. It's important to understand and accept your child's current developmental stage rather than expecting them to act like an adult.

Therefore, rearing children is an opportunity to stretch, to look beyond your current beliefs. In so doing, you choose to discard the beliefs, thoughts, and values that cause separation and suffering for you and those around you. Instead, you invite in those beliefs, thoughts, and values that create a family rooted in mutual support and growth.

My perspective on child rearing is deeply influenced by being raised in the United States during the 1950s, 1960s, and 70s and attending the University of California at Berkeley. I studied psychology and education and began practicing Buddhism.

I often read the Lebanese artist, philosopher, and writer Kahlil Gibran's book, *The Prophet*. I was profoundly touched by his poem, "On Children."

On Children

Your children are not your children.
They are the sons and daughters of Life's longing for itself.
They come through you but not from you,
And though they are with you, yet they belong not to you.
You may give them your love but not your thoughts,
For they have their own thoughts.
You may house their bodies but not their souls,
For their souls dwell in the house of tomorrow,
which you cannot visit, not even in your dreams.
You may strive to be like them, but seek not to make them
    like you.
For life goes not backward nor tarries with yesterday.
You are the bows from which your children as living
    arrows are sent forth.
The archer sees the mark upon the path of the infinite,
    and he bends you with his might that his arrows may
    go swift and far.Let your bending in the archer's hand
    be for gladness;
For even as he loves the arrow that flies, so he loves also
    the bow that is stable.

In my view, a great parent is someone who continuously self-reflects about their parenting and makes ongoing changes. Here are some self-reflective questions to help you uncover the source(s) of parent-child problems you may be facing so you can then discover effective solutions:

- Am I taking time to sit and listen to my child without interrupting and giving advice?

- What am I saying that is making my child stop talking to me?

- Am I trying to control my child by making him "suffer" in order to change his behavior?

- Why do I hang on to punishing my child? Can I let go of the erroneous belief that a suffering child will be more cooperative in the future?

- Am I afraid of losing my "sense of power"?

- Am I trying to change myself or my child?

- Why do I keep my negative behavior cycle going? What do I get out of it?

- What feelings are being triggered from my own childhood?

- Am I clear on what rules are negotiable and non-negotiable?

- Am I trying to figure out how my child can get their needs met in a positive way instead of taking their behavior as a personal affront?

- Do I know how my child needs to mature in order to gain new freedoms from me?

- Am I looking at my child's growth as a process that takes time?

- Am I developing the patience needed to become a compassionate parent who loves unconditionally? Am I working on diffusing and changing my angry reactions?

- Am I forgiving myself when I make a poor decision and trying again?

When parents view children as their possessions, subject to the parental authority of pushing and prodding to become what parents want, parents miss the opportunity for personal growth that raising children offers. I realize some cultures believe that ensuring their children's financial success is equivalent to ensuring their bright future. American children, in particular, are raised to believe in the inherent freedom of will and thought. This belief makes it very difficult for authoritarian style parents to raise children here in the United States.

What children crave and appreciate from their parents, above all else, is acknowledgement for who they are, much more so than what parents do for them or give to them. The mutual appreciation of one another and sharing life experiences together are at the heart of a joyful parent-child relationship.

When parents prioritize this relationship above the demands of their hectic lives and busy schedules, they have the opportunity to enjoy their children instead of managing them. Just as parents want to highlight positive behavior, we also want to give greater attention to the positive experiences of life with our children. Look for positivity not only in the happy times, but also in the joy that is often created through overcoming challenges together.

I offer a roadmap for how to shift from being an authoritarian adversary to a guiding ally. As an ally, you still set rules and expectations to protect and steer children. The difference is that you also learn how to listen to their unique thoughts and emotions as you teach them how to solve problems, both together and on their own, so that they can create a successful life.

7.
Your Childhood Impacts Your Parenting

As parents, we all have visions of how we want to interact with our kids and how we want them to respond. No one wants to yell, threaten, shame, feel powerless, hurt, or give up. So, why is it so difficult for us to realize our visions?

During childhood, each of us developed beliefs about ourselves and about the roles of parents and children. These beliefs and values seemingly seeped into our pores without us consciously analyzing or choosing them. Our prefrontal cortex, also known as the logical brain, was in an early developmental stage, so most of our learning was done on an unconscious level in the limbic system, which is the emotional center of the brain.

When interacting with your kids, your childhood emotions can suddenly be triggered without even realizing it. These old emotions don't wave a flag and say, "This is old stuff, and it doesn't relate to what's happening now." Instead, these old, intense feelings can erupt, feel valid, and direct your actions. You may suddenly sound and act just like your parents.

Unless we analyze our intense reactions and discover whether a memory is being triggered, we'll end up feeling controlled by our kids and our emotions. We'll blame our kids for our upsets and say they're manipulating us, trying to push our buttons, or simply out to get us.

Blaming your children creates a victim mentality that leaves parents powerless to transform negative situations. Seeing your kids as the problem to fix leads you to use controlling parenting strategies through which you try to change your kids rather than change yourself. A key component of changing yourself involves understanding the reasons behind your feelings and actions.

I recommend using the evaluation process of the Think-Feel-Do Cycle by Michael Popkin. Read Chapter 14, *The Key to Making Positive Parenting Changes Stick*, in Section 3, to better understand yourself and to make better choices.

Let's say that your vision is to have a family where everyone shares their thoughts and feelings without fear of being judged or criticized. If you experienced this family atmosphere as a child, then you already have an ingrained model to follow. If you're having a hard time creating this supportive environment, then it's important to examine the critical and judgmental childhood messages and language you learned and are now repeating.

For example, if, as a child, you heard judgmental statements such as, "You should have known," then it can be very difficult to hear helpful suggestions from your partner or children because the childhood inner voice of, *I should have known*, gets triggered. As a result, you believe that you have to defend your "all-knowing" position. This erroneous belief often leads to getting defensive and angry, which creates a wall between you and your loved ones. Your children and partner are likely afraid to tell you what they think and feel, and your defensive beliefs keep you from realizing your dream of having a close and connected family.

I was raised with, "You should have," and it led me to use power and control in my personal and parenting lives. Luckily, I had a strong-willed daughter who didn't respond well to this approach. My vision for a close and connected relationship with her, even through the teen years, was the driving force behind my self-reflection and change. Once I acknowledged my need to be right, I consciously chose to say to myself, *It's okay to not know everything. I'm still valuable and important. I can learn from others and become better because of their help.*

Take some time to write down what you learned during childhood about yourself and about how parents are to be treated. What words did you often hear that are now causing you to be triggered by your children's words and actions? Perhaps you heard, "Children should be seen and not heard," "Don't talk back," "Respect your elders," "I'm the adult so listen to what I say," "Do as you're told," "Be respectful," "Don't argue with me," "How many times do I have to…," etc. Maybe you learned to take responsibility for the feelings of others every time you heard, "You make me so mad," "If you just behaved, I wouldn't get mad," "It's your fault."

To realize your family vision, it is crucial to be able to remain in the moment so you can listen openly to your children and partner's thoughts and feelings. I encourage you to find a support person who can help you unravel your childhood triggers so you can gain greater power over yourself and respond to your loved ones in a positive manner.

8.
Choose Your Parental Role:
Director, Collaborator, or Supporter

In order to guide our children toward success, it's essential to understand our role in each challenge we encounter with them. There are essentially three parenting roles that you will choose from depending on whether the parent, parent and child together, or only the child will decide how to solve the problem.

1. **The Director:** Sets rules, guidelines, and expectations

2. **The Collaborator:** Discusses challenges with children and decides on solutions together

3. **The Supporter/Confidant:** Supports children's own problem-solving process where the child makes the final decision

Unless we clearly understand which parenting role to adopt, we risk being either too lax or too controlling in our children's lives. Our parenting role is directly connected to who "owns" the problem. The process I use to determine the appropriate parenting role for each challenge is based on the problem ownership questions developed by Dr. Michael Popkin.

The questions are as follows:

1. Who brings up the problem and wants to find a solution to their unmet goals or needs?

2. Does the problem involve health, safety, family rules, or values?

3. If the problem is for the child to solve, is the problem solvable within reasonable limits for the child's age and level of maturity?

Here are some further guidelines for each parenting role with common examples for each role. Your role will vary as you evaluate each challenge based on your child's age, ability, personality, needs, and situational factors. Many issues exist in more than one parenting role category due to these child-related factors. Regardless of parenting role, flexibility and open-mindedness are key to interacting successfully with your children.

The Director: When you bring up a concern your child doesn't see as their problem, and it involves health, safety, rules, or values, then the problem directly affects only you. Until your kids embrace your values, which may not be until adulthood, your parental role is to decide how your concern will be addressed. Chores often fall into this category unless you have a child who loves to help. You can choose to either direct what each child does or problem solve together. Either way, you will need to be the rule enforcer to make sure your requests are being met. Unfortunately, parents often get angry when they have to remind their kids. When you accept your role as a Director without getting angry, everyone will be happier. Then, you can direct using effective strategies with warmth, and your kids' resistance will diminish.

Examples: The parent owns the problem. Issues include refusal to do homework or chores, bad language, friends, hitting, anger, allowance, etc. Also, follow-through of morning and afternoon routines after a plan is developed.

The Collaborator: When your child is complaining about a family member, teacher, friend, etc., you need to ask follow-up questions to determine whether the problem is your child's to solve or a problem to be solved together. Ask yourself question #2 from the problem ownership questions listed previously: Does the problem involve health, safety, rules, or values? If it does, then you probably need to problem solve together by brainstorming ideas and agreeing on the final solution. The Collaborator does less enforcing than the Director because the child has a vested interest in fixing the problem.

Examples: The parent and child/teen own the problem together. Issues include the child waking up late, fighting with siblings, problems with teachers that the child can't handle on his own, bullying, when new freedoms are given, anger (if it's impacting the family), and problems with homework, dating, money, friends, etc.

The Supporter/Confidant: If your child is sharing a problem or making a complaint and it doesn't involve health, safety, rules, or values, then ask yourself question #3 from the list above: Is my child mature enough to take care of the problem with only my support in finding a solution? If so, you won't tell her what to do or take action on her behalf. Your role will be that of a Supporter who is available to discuss the problem, if requested. Learning the problem-solving process is crucial to being "hired" as a Supporter by your children. In the Supporter Role, you are able to discuss the problem with your child until the solution-finding step, as long as you keep in mind that the child makes the final decision without your influence. If your child doesn't want to discuss their final decision with you, then you embrace the Confidant Role which is a reduced version of the Supporter Role. The distinction between Supporter and Confidant is further elaborated in Section 5, which is the problem-solving section of this book.

Examples: The child/teen owns the problem. Issues include friendship problems, the child valuing homework and requesting help, decisions about the future, challenges with teachers where the teacher is open to dialogue and the child/teen feels powerful enough to approach the teacher, the child's own anger (if it is not impacting the family), problems with love and money, etc.

Keep in mind that as your children mature, you will collaborate on issues that you once directed. With increased maturity on the part of your children, your main role will be that of the Supporter/Confidant. If you continue to direct your kids in a way that hinders their individuation process, they may become angry with you, rebel against your control, and refuse to do what you want. This is a warning sign for you to step back, reevaluate who really owns the problem, and choose the correct parental role to maintain a healthy relationship with your kids.

Section 2

Creating Open Communication

9.
The Emotional Support Process Connects You to Your Child

The Emotional Support Process (E.S.P.) is a set of essential parenting skills that creates open communication and influence with your child. Through the E.S.P., you guide your child from an emotional, stuck state to a logical, creative state. The skills involved include an awareness and avoidance of blocking communication, empathetic listening and speaking, problem-solving discussions, and supportive dialogue. These skills are taught throughout Ally Parenting.

The diagram of the E.S.P. is comprised of five panels that describe your child's emotional states and needs as well as ways for you to respond effectively so that your child can express their upset and move toward a more rational state. Instead of labeling the figures in the diagram as "child" and "adult," I have called them "speaker" and "listener" because this process is applicable to all relationships, whether between you and your partner, friend, parent, co-worker, or even boss. When you master the E.S.P., you can improve all relationships.

Depending on your child's nature, their expression of feelings may range from intense displays to refusal to acknowledge you. No matter where your child falls on this emotional continuum or which parenting role you're using, the Emotional Support Process will allow you to bridge the gap that forms between you and your child during conflicts or their personal upsets. As you practice the E.S.P., you will win their trust and become their ally.

We are born emotional beings, and there's no way to avoid emotions as they are how we connect with others. Our limbic system, the emotional brain, is developed before birth, whereas our prefrontal cortex, the logical brain, starts developing after birth.

As such, your children need you to learn how to respond effectively to their emotions right from the start. The E.S.P. gives you the skills to feel confident when emotions arise. Through the E.S.P., you will know how to respond so that emotions can be released, you won't be triggered, and better thinking can arise.

Often, parents want to avoid emotional upsets, so they try to calm their child, dismiss them, get angry at them, or numerous other approaches that make the situation worse. This is called blocking communication, which will be covered later in this section in the chapters, *Awareness of Communication Blocks is the First Step* and *Why Kids Reject Our Help – and How to Win Their Trust*.

In the chapters, *Empathy Improves Connection and Communication* and *Parent Success Stories of Using Empathetic Responses*, you will learn how to listen with empathy rather than block communication. When you listen and respond with empathetic phrases, your child talks more about their feelings and thoughts, thus giving them greater clarity and decision-making ability. When you learn how to avoid blocking communication, you will increase your child's self-expression. This will enable you to be more empathetic, nonjudgmental, supportive, compassionate, understanding, flexible, collaborative, open-minded, and encouraging with your children and others. Your enhanced parent-child connections will create a solid foundation for weathering future storms, especially during the teen years.

As you learn the E.S.P., it's also important to learn the necessary skills for each parenting role in order to be an effective Director, Collaborator, or Supporter. It's like riding a bike. The E.S.P. is the back wheel, and the parenting strategy you've chosen is the front wheel. As you turn both wheels, you become more skilled at moving forward, steering, and balancing, so you can lead your family toward successful interactions. Just as becoming a confident bike rider requires learning new skills and trusting your teacher, the more you practice the E.S.P. and your strategies, the more confident you will become as you witness your successes.

I admit that the E.S.P. is not easy, especially if you weren't listened to by an adult during your own childhood. Combining the E.S.P. with a Director Role or problem-solving strategy may feel uncomfortable and not "parental" at first. You may resist learning how to support your child emotionally because you believe that you're being too soft, you need to stop your child's upset, or your child will assume they'll get their way if they're listened to. These are common misconceptions that will be disproven as soon as you begin the E.S.P.

My goal is to teach you how to use the Emotional Support Process so that you can experience its amazing benefits and understand its essential role in being your child's ally rather than their adversary. When you provide the emotional support that your child needs, you dissolve walls of conflict and instead build bridges of understanding and lifelong connections.

In order to become an empathetic Supporter, you will need to self-reflect, reveal your hidden beliefs, and examine them logically under a microscope of clarity. It is helpful to discuss the concepts in this book with other parents so you can help each other identify the thoughts and beliefs that are clouding your ability to be emotionally available and supportive to your children. When I learned the brain science of feelings and practiced supporting my upset daughter, my lack of understanding and helpless feelings during her upsets disappeared, and a beautiful bond of closeness took its place. My desire is for you to experience the same benefits as I did.

Emotional Support Process

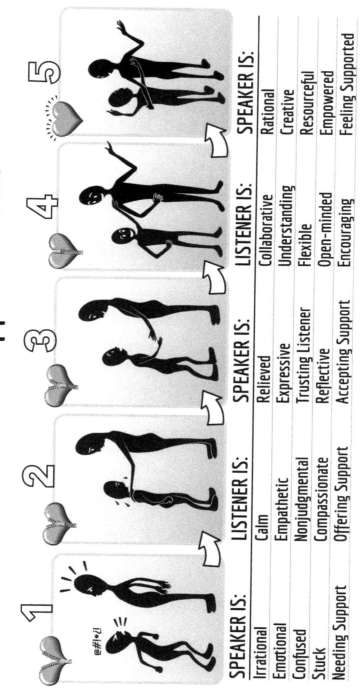

	1	2	3	4	5
	SPEAKER IS:	LISTENER IS:	SPEAKER IS:	LISTENER IS:	SPEAKER IS:
	Irrational	Calm	Relieved	Collaborative	Rational
	Emotional	Empathetic	Expressive	Understanding	Creative
	Confused	Nonjudgmental	Trusting Listener	Flexible	Resourceful
	Stuck	Compassionate	Reflective	Open-minded	Empowered
	Needing Support	Offering Support	Accepting Support	Encouraging	Feeling Supported

10.
Awareness of Communication Blocks Is the First Step

Parents rarely try to shut down their kids. We want them to talk with us. We are often confused when our words and attitudes break down communication and everyone becomes upset. We wonder what's happening. Without our awareness, our words suddenly feel hurtful to our kids, and they either get very angry with us or stop talking. Our loving ally relationship suddenly becomes adversarial.

Michael Popkin, PhD, states that a communication block is any remark or attitude on the part of the listener (the parent) that injures the self-esteem of the speaker (the child) to the extent that communication breaks down. When you feel an emotional wall go up between you and your child where one didn't exist before, something you said or did was likely a communication block.

Depending on their age and personality, children respond differently to words. The timing of words can also change their impact from negative to positive. For example, advice given early in a conversation might be considered unwanted, whereas advice shared after the child feels heard and understood could feel like helpful support.

Everything you learn about communication blocks with children is applicable to communication with adults as well. Avoiding communication blocks is not a secret weapon to get your kids to talk. Rather, it is an essential skill for all family members to learn in order to create a caring, cooperative, and courageous family together. Show your kids what you're learning and bravely ask them to identify your communication blocks, particularly the ones they want you to stop doing first. Refrain from telling them to stop their own blocks. That will come in time. Now is the time for you to change.

Children are often accused of being the cause of family arguments. Too often, parents think, *If only my kid would just cooperate and not get angry, everything would be fine.* When you understand how you are blocking communication, you take responsibility for changing your family dynamics. Simply by telling your kids that you are working on communicating better, they will be more caring and respectful toward you. Not being blamed as the problem takes a huge burden off their shoulders. As the parent, you have the maturity to change the most.

In the Communication Blocks chart there are four columns. The first column labels the name of the block, the second provides the underlying intention of the words, the third explains the hurtful message the child hears, and the fourth gives examples of how the blocking sentences often start. As you read the examples, think of the words you say so you can understand which blocks you use and why your child feels hurt.

COMMUNICATION BLOCKS	PARENT'S INTENTION	WHAT IT REALLY SAYS TO THE CHILD/TEEN	EXAMPLES
Commanding	To control the situation and provide the child with quick solutions	"You don't have the right to decide how to handle your own problems"	"What you should do is..." "Stop complaining."
Giving Advice	To influence the child with arguments or opinions	"You don't have the good sense to come up with your own solutions."	"I've got a good idea..." "Why don't you..."
Placating	To take away the child's pain; to make her feel better	"You don't have a right to your feelings; you can't handle discomfort."	"It isn't as bad as it seems." "Everything will be okay."
Interrogating	To get to the bottom of the problem and find out what the child did wrong	"You must have messed up somewhere."	"What did you do to him?"
Distracting	To protect the child from the problem by changing the subject	"I don't think you can stand the discomfort long enough to find a real solution."	"Let's not worry about that, let's..."
Psychologizing	To help prevent future problems by analyzing the child's behavior and explaining his motives	"I know more about you than you know about yourself. So I'm superior to you."	"Do you know why you said that?"
Sarcasm	To show the child how wrong her attitudes or behavior are by making her feel ridiculous	"You are ridiculous."	"Well, I guess that's just about the end of the world."
Moralizing	To show the child the proper way to deal with the problem	"Don't you dare choose your own values."	"The right thing to do would be to..." "Oh, how awful."
Know-It-All	To show the child that he has a resource for handling any problem, namely, the parent	"Since I know it all, you must know nothing."	"The solution is really very simple."
Me-Tooism	To show the child that you understand and can give advice	"My experience is more important to talk about now."	"I had that happen to me when I was your age."

11.
Empathy Improves Connection and Communication

Children's emotions can often surge and be difficult for them to understand and for us to handle. Loving, lasting, and meaningful relationships are built during these emotional moments. When we connect with our children during stressful, "out-of- control," or even reflective times, we teach them that we value them and their emotions. We demonstrate that we understand and can manage our own emotions and that, with time, they can manage themselves, as well.

Children's higher-level thinking, the prefrontal cortex, doesn't fully develop until their mid 20s. Therefore, their ability to have reflective emotional self-control is very minimal when they are young and develops with brain maturation and our guidance. It can be difficult to be around and listen to your upset children if you were not listened to as a child or if old hurts are stimulated. Getting support in sorting out your childhood feelings will allow you to be more present and accepting with your children.

I like to use the analogy of a pressure cooker to describe the emotional or limbic system in the brain. When a pressure cooker heats up to a boil, it needs to release steam through the pressure release valve or it will explode. You have probably seen your child become more and more upset, like an overheated pressure cooker, who explodes either verbally, physically, or both.

When you respond to strong emotions in ways that your child takes as communication blocks, you are holding down the emotional release valve, causing the emotions to keep intensifying and being expressed outwardly or inwardly. Your erroneous attempts to calm your child cause more inner strife because right now your child needs to feel heard, not squelched.

The greatest gift you can offer your children during upsets is an accepting listening ear. The result of your love, connection, and giving time to release emotions is a child who afterwards can think more flexibly, creatively, and cooperatively. Listening openly is the second step of the problem-solving process and will be discussed later. To better understand this process, think of your personal experiences of feeling emotionally overloaded, being able to release these emotions, and then feeling and acting more yourself afterwards. It is similar for children.

Parents can create a wall when they use a communication block after their child shares their upset feelings or complains about something in their life. The child trusts the parent and tries to seek their support and help. Instead of offering the desired support with empathy, the parent responds with a communication block, such as giving unwanted advice, interrogating, commanding, or placating.

Since the parent is responsible for creating the immediate wall, mending this type of poor connection is easier than when the child won't share at all. Improved connection is created when you learn the skill of using empathetic responses during emotional moments rather than a communication block. You can shift away from blocking to reconnecting by saying, "I'm sorry. What I said wasn't helpful. I want to hear what you have to say. I won't tell you what to do. Please continue."

A more challenging wall that parents encounter is their child's inability or unwillingness to share what's troubling them. A child may be embarrassed about their thoughts and feelings, what has happened to them, or what their parents will think about them if they share. This embarrassment builds an inner wall of silence and disconnection, which leads parents to worry and feel helpless.

Because of their deep caring, parents seek ways to build a bridge of connection so their child will feel safe and be willing to open up to them. When you respond with an empathetic phrase, such as, "It seems like something is wrong," or "You look pretty upset right now," or "I'm here to just listen to you without judgment," you start to build a bridge of trust.

The wall of silence is the scariest, yet it can be melted gradually as you perfect your empathetic listening and phrasing. Your child may also want their own professional to talk to as you improve your communication skills. To change, first engage in a thorough examination of your past responses to your child as they shared their thoughts and feelings with you. Self-reflection is the beginning step to using empathetic phrases effectively. You will probably need help with this process because it entails writing down what you usually say and determining which communication blocks you tend to use. Don't blame your child for closing herself off from you. Instead, take full responsibility for determining your part in building the wall between you and your child. Having the courage to self-reflect will inspire your child to do the same.

Most kids feel blamed for not talking to their parents. Because you are owning responsibility for the wall between the two of you, you are taking guilt off of your child's shoulders and putting it onto your own. You are giving your child the wonderful gift of relief and emotional support that they desperately need from you.

Once you've written down examples of your usual responses and their corresponding communication blocks, ask your child for permission to share what you've discovered. "I've been thinking about how I've hurt your feelings when you've wanted to share with me. I'm learning about what I'm probably doing wrong. I'd like to know what you think."

Depending on your child's maturity level and depth of hurt, their response will range from, "I don't know," to "Yeah. You're always telling me what to do and I don't like it. You're also always talking about yourself. I wish you'd stop." Your response, "You're right. Which one or two of the blocks do you want me to work on stopping first?" If your words aren't melting the wall yet, try writing a letter about the blocks, what changes you want to make, and that you value their input and advice. Then, let them come to you.

Every parent-child relationship is different, so there's no "right" way to approach a child. My ideas are meant to serve as a springboard for finding what's best for you. You could also say to your child, "I've been thinking about how I usually respond to you when you're upset, and I think I've figured out some reasons why you don't want to talk with me. I'd like to share my thoughts, and when you're ready, I'd also like to hear what you think about this. Would you be willing to listen to me for ten minutes?"

Your vulnerability is the key to your kids' learning to trust you again. If they answer "no" to the question above, don't get hurt and defensive. They are responding that way because they're so hurt by you that they want to hurt you back. Think to yourself, *It's going to take time to tear down the wall I helped build. I can handle this.* You can then say to your child, "Okay, I'll leave what I've written down and check in with you later to see if you've changed your mind. I love you, and it's important to me to fix our relationship." Then, continue to work on not blocking communication in future interactions so your child will trust that you are truly trying to change.

The purpose of the empathetic responses is to guide your child through their emotional state, where the limbic system is overflowing, to the logical state so they can solve problems. No one can solve problems when they are emotional and you can't tell someone, "Don't be emotional." That will make them more upset. Instead, learn what empathetic responses encourage the release of emotions which may first come out unintelligible, and then eventually more understandable, and then logical. It's important that your child feels connected, heard, and safe. Emotional connection builds trust and rapport and will keep your child sharing and, possibly, open to problem solving together in the future.

Some children like having their feelings validated while others find talking about their feelings too intimate. The latter thinker types prefer third person or abstract empathetic wording in order to feel safe. You will discover the best approach for each child through trial and error. When you speak in a way that blocks communication, simply apologize and try again. You can implement your new communication skills with other family members and friends as well.

When deciding what to say, listen for the feelings and meaning behind your child's words. Your goal is to respond so that your child feels safe to continue talking, crying, and expressing their feelings. Your intention is not to be right or judgmental, rather to provide unconditional support and love so that your child trusts you and feels accepted for whatever they are saying or feeling. Be careful not to say "but" after an empathetic response or explain what you think your child "should" change. Allow your empathy to be truly felt through your words as well as your silence. Empathetic listening is the second step of the Emotional Support Process.

Parents often easily confuse reflective listening with empathetic listening. These two types of listening are not the same, and each has a different purpose. Reflective listening is a communication skill in which the listener seeks to understand the speaker's idea and then offers the idea back to the speaker to confirm that it has been understood correctly. Reflective listening can be used during the problem-solving process, but is not helpful when emotions are being vented. Responding with logic when your child is emotional will upset them and create a communication block.

The more you practice, the more you will discover what words, or omission of words, keep the conversation flowing. Continue to use empathetic comments, not questions, until your child's emotions have been released. Sometimes, problem solving together will follow, and then you can ask questions.

Here are some empathetic comments to try:

"That sounds like a real problem."

"It's hard to know what to do."

"I understand why you don't want to…"

"I can see why you're upset, mad, disappointed, discouraged, humiliated, etc."

"It looks like this is really stressing you out."

"You seem overwhelmed, upset, unhappy, determined, etc."

"I think you'd rather be doing something more fun right now."

"Yeah, Algebra has never been your favorite subject."

"It can be hard to go through what you're experiencing right now."

"I'm interested in what you have to say. I can give you my total attention for... minutes."

"That seems really hard, difficult, challenging, frustrating, almost impossible, etc."

"I'm sorry to hear that."

"Mmm, I see."

"I'm here for you. You're safe with me."

It's important for your responses not to feel manipulative. At first, it will feel awkward to be empathetic if you're used to giving advice, interrogating, or using other communication blocks. With time and practice, you will develop heartfelt responses because you'll experience the joy of feeling emotionally connected with and supportive of your children and partner. Share the skill of listening openly with empathetic phrases with all family members. Instead of telling others to change, work on your own communication skills, and they will follow your lead.

12.
Why Kids Reject Our Help – and How to Win Their Trust

Children usually reject our help because we are using communication blocks. What we consider helping words feel like hurting words to our child. This is not our intention. When I first learned about communication blocks (remarks that hurt your child's self-esteem and shut down communication) as an Active Parenting course instructor, my life changed. I realized that if I didn't take responsibility for my daughter's, husband's, and other people's negative reactions to what I said, I wouldn't be able to improve my relationships. The more I took responsibility for learning how to build bridges to better understanding rather than blocks to communication, the more I could create connected and close interactions.

My deep, intense desire to have a close relationship with my daughter after it became rocky during her early adolescence is what motivated me to change. I was determined that my daughter would not feel the suffering I felt as a teenager due to not having a close and trusting relationship with my mother.

Any change requires self-reflection as well as a motivating force to drive you through the unpleasantness of acknowledging the need to change, trying new ideas, failing, and then trying again until you succeed. What is your motivation to change? Perhaps your driving force is, as mine was, the vision of a happier and more cooperative family.

The core of many family problems I encounter is a lack of knowledge about what people, including ourselves, need when they're upset. Dr. Michael Popkin clearly explains how we hurt others when we block communication by giving unwanted advice, commanding, interrogating, or using the other blocks, rather than listening with empathy. In these situations, your child often rejects your well-meaning advice.

It takes courage, self-awareness, and skill to listen openly to a suffering child without trying to eliminate her pain in some way. Instead of making a child feel better, your loving "help" can have the opposite effect. Your attempts at fixing can make children feel undervalued, unimportant, and unsupported, the exact opposite of what you want. Your choice of words and actions can turn into unintentional barriers to communication rather than bridges to understanding.

Before we can stop blocking communication and instead listen openly, we need to recognize the defensive emotional reactions that keep us from focusing on what our child is feeling, thinking, and needing from us in the moment. When we are defensive, we interpret our child's resistance to our fixing as a rejection. Rather than focusing on how we can help our child cope with her feelings and thoughts, we can become self-focused on how to protect our own hurt feelings.

The need to protect ourselves when we feel hurt can be expressed through revenge. It's tough to acknowledge the vengeful words, feelings, and actions that shut down loving and helpful communication. Once we start defending ourselves, we create an adversarial relationship in which no one ends up feeling good. It's up to us to stop the hurt, connect emotionally with our kids' needs, and offer meaningful problem-solving communication.

Here is an example of how a negative, defensive interaction might play out:

Situation: Your child is struggling with homework, and you want to help so they don't keep suffering. You decide to give advice. Often, children don't want advice because the hurtful underlying message is that they can't find their own solutions. Your advice, regardless of your intention, is perceived as a communication block or barrier.

Parent's advice: "I think you should work on your homework for 30 minutes, take a 10-minute break, and then work on it for 30 more minutes."

Hurt child's possible responses: "I'm not going to do that. I'll never get it done if I do it that way. You don't understand. You think I'm stupid."

Triggered parent's possible thoughts: *She thinks I'm stupid. She's rejecting my idea. She never listens to me. My older siblings never listened to me. Everyone always told me to shut up. She's so mean. I'm not going to help her anymore. She's a spoiled and ungrateful child.*

Triggered parent's possible defensive responses: "I wasn't saying you're stupid. Don't be so sensitive. I'm just trying to help. Don't talk to me that way. We don't allow that kind of language in our house. That's disrespectful. You can just do it on your own, then. Don't blame me if you fail. You are so unappreciative of everything I do for you. I would never have spoken to my parents the way you talk to me."

Hurt child's possible response: "I hate you. Why are you so mean? Leave me alone. I didn't ask for your help. You don't understand. I hate my life."

The continual breakdown of communication can lead to yelling, crying, slamming doors, tantrums, isolation, and more hurtful words. You have the power to change this negative dynamic in your family. Change begins with your determination to shift your triggered thoughts and defensive responses. When you take control of your emotional center and engage your logical brain, you not only create more positive interactions with your kids, you also teach them how to become more emotionally aware and intelligent.

Let's say that you gave unwanted advice, which is why your child wouldn't listen to you, and your child responded with hurtful comments. You realize your mistake and want to reverse the hurt since you didn't avoid it from the beginning. Here's how to respond as a supportive parent:

Parent's thoughts: *I've hurt her feelings. She just wants to be listened to right now. She doesn't need my advice.*

Parent's response: "I'm sorry. You don't need my advice. You're feeling really bad about your homework right now."

Child's response: "It's horrible. I just can't do it, and I'm not going to. They give way too much homework."

Parent's response: "I bet you would rather be doing anything but homework right now."

Child's response: "Yeah! I'd love to watch a movie and forget about all of my work."

Parent's response: "I know."

Child's response: "It just isn't fair. Why do they give so much homework?"

Parent's response: "That's definitely something to think and talk about. What about tonight, though?"

Child's response: "I know I have to do it, but I just don't know how to do it all."

Parent's response: "What if we talk about ideas together and come up with a solution to try?"

Child's response: "Okay, thanks."

When parents understand the steps required for change, they have two reactions. The first is a wave of hope, relief, and confidence because they finally know why they're having problems with their kids. The second is a sense of being overwhelmed because there is so much to learn and change. Parents often say, "It's going to be really hard for me to change."

If you're feeling this way, too, know that small changes by you can create huge positive changes in your children.

As you work on eliminating your hurtful communication blocks, you will then learn how to respond empathetically. Your careful listening and responding tells your children that you care about them and so your children will care about what you say in return. As a result, your child will share more, and be more willing to listen to your advice and perhaps even act on it.

13.
Parent Success Stories of Using Empathetic Responses

Parents Work Together as a Winning Team

We participated in private parenting coaching with Cynthia, and as a result, we've experienced greater harmony together as parents. Since we have the same parenting approach now, it feels like we're working as a team to face our child-rearing challenges. Our relationship as a couple has also improved.

Here are our personal experiences of learning effective new skills for parenting our 8-year-old daughter.

Mother: Participating in private parenting education training with Cynthia has given my husband and me a unified approach to raising our sensitive child together. Understanding communication blocks has been helpful in improving our relationship with one another as well as with our daughter.

One of my main goals for our coaching with Cynthia was to reduce my upsets with my daughter, which I'm happy to report I've been able to do.

Cynthia has taught me to understand my daughter more and to listen to her emotions rather than argue with her and try to control her. My daughter and I have also created ways in which she can manage her own frustrations before they get out of control. I feel much happier about the way I'm interacting with my daughter, and I will continue to use the parenting tools Cynthia has taught us.

Father: One of my main goals for working with Cynthia was to improve my daughter's behavior and have her show respect by listening more to adults. I realized that I would use logic to try to get her to change, which wasn't working.

Cynthia taught me the importance of listening to and acknowledging my daughter's emotions first. Doing so has improved my connection with her. My daughter is still challenging, yet I am focusing on how I can interact with her more effectively to help bring out better responses from her.

Special Time and Empathy Create an Agreeable 5-Year-Old Son

My husband and I came to Cynthia because of our high-spirited and creative son who hates time limits and doing what he is told.

We struggle with every daily activity. We discussed the goals of behavior with Cynthia and realized that our son is getting connection and power through undue attention seeking and rebellion rather than through cooperation and independence.

We had gotten into negative reactions with him that has caused a vicious cycle. We decided to focus on connecting with him first thing in the morning through giving him attention and positive power. We set the timer for five minutes and he directs the play to do whatever he wants with one of us. We don't do video games or watch T.V. Just fun together creating laughter.

I was worried that when the timer went off, he would have a tantrum. Instead, he just groaned, and I said, "We're having fun. We'll do it again tomorrow." Then he was fine and we had the best morning ever. He was actually agreeable. Just five minutes of him being in control of playtime with us filled his need for power and connection in a positive way. We'll keep doing devoted play each morning. Thanks, Cynthia.

Dad Stays Quiet So Teen Talks More

My wife and I recently started the month-long Accelerated Wisdom Program with Cynthia.

We came to Cynthia primarily to open up communication with our 13-year-old daughter. She wasn't telling us much about what she was thinking or feeling, and that was a concern due to the many potential issues teens face.

At the end of our initial four-hour session, I was astonished to realize that what I thought were empathetic and encouraging comments were actually keeping our daughter from talking.

I would say things that apparently felt like an interrogation or were about me rather than her. I learned that these are two communication blocks called interrogating and me-tooism.

I knew that what I was doing wasn't the best, but I didn't know why or what to do instead. Cynthia totally understood my communication errors. I left our first session focused on stopping myself so that our daughter would have space to talk.

That week, our daughter came home and told us that she wanted to drop a class at school. I wanted to cut her off and jump in with my ideas and a story about myself, which would have shut her down in the past. Instead, I remembered that I needed to give her space to talk, so I stopped. I just said, "Okay," in a non-committal way.

I was amazed that our daughter kept talking! I was even able to say that we could talk about it more later and help her make a decision, if she wanted.

My awareness and willingness to try Cynthia's advice has made me feel closer to our daughter. I think she will learn to trust me more and share more as I keep practicing listening openly without judgment, interrupting her, or talking about myself.

Thank you so much, Cynthia. Your wisdom is amazing, and you give us the exact guidance we need.

Mom Truly Hears Her Son For the First Time

Dear Cynthia,

You have made me aware of how to listen carefully to my 12-year-old son and not diminish his feelings. In some ways, I feel like I'm truly hearing him for the first time. I regret all the time I spent not listening to him.

There are years of miscommunication to correct. I'm much more conscious of how I talk to him now and even what I say, and I'm trying hard not to "badger" him or flood him with requests. We still struggle with organization, his strong will to do as he pleases at bedtime, and how much screen time he wants.

One result of truly listening to my son is that we allowed him to quit one of his activities after four years. He's showing more interest in physical challenges now, so we enrolled him in judo/jujitsu instead. In contrast to the lack of attention and praise he was given in his previous activity, his current teachers have noticed his physical talent and have focused extra attention on helping him accomplish the moves he's trying to perfect. It's so nice to see a teacher finally notice my son and give him accolades for his efforts.

You have made me aware that listening to my son will help guide us toward to his true passions and nurture his true self. We know that this is the path to joy for anyone, and we really want that for him in his life.

I've enjoyed working with you, Cynthia. You knew how to ask the right questions to get to the heart of the parenting issues I faced. I intend to review the information you shared with me and hear your voice in my head saying, *Think about whether what you say will connect you to or alienate you from your child.* Now, I always tell parents to say to themselves, *Will what I am about to say or do build up or break down my relationship with my child?* Thank you so much for your wisdom and encouragement, Cynthia.

Mom Learns to Worry Less and Listen More to Teen

My husband and I have an 18-year-old son, and it feels like I'm constantly worrying about him. As a result, I had become over-controlling, and my son doesn't want to be a "mama's boy." I decided that I needed help from Cynthia to stop the worrying and to improve my communication skills.

The primary skill I'm practicing is avoiding the communication blocks of giving advice, commanding, and me-tooism, which is when I talk about myself too much. Here's a story of how I'm improving.

My husband, son, and I recently rented kayaks at the Russian River. My husband and son started out in the same kayak. My husband hasn't been training with Cynthia as I have, so he started telling my son that he wasn't paddling right.

I could see that the situation was deteriorating quickly and that my son's feelings were being hurt, so I asked my son to share my kayak with me. I didn't direct him, so he felt in control of the kayak. He was giving me directions, instead of the other way around, and he loved it.

While reporting this success to Cynthia, we discussed how I could have gone further to the second step of problem solving, which is to listen openly to my son's feelings.

I could've acknowledged my son's feelings once he was in my kayak by saying, "I know it's hard to listen to Dad." This statement would have made him feel understood and possibly led to more dialogue and problem solving about his challenges with his father.

Recently, on several occasions, I was talking to my son about choices, the car, and looking for a job. I would start telling him what to do, and then I would realize that I was using a communication block. When I noticed this, I stopped myself and started saying, "You have a really good head on your shoulders, and I'm sure you'll come up with a good solution."

Cynthia is now encouraging me to take on the Supporter Role of problem solving together rather than telling my son that he can solve his problems on his own.

This is a entirely new way of thinking for me, and it's taking me a while to learn. I'm doing well with the first step of being aware of the communication blocks that cause me to be too directive. I'm either avoiding them completely, or shifting quickly and stopping once I realize I'm blocking communication, as I see the negative results.

The next step is to keep perfecting the skill of listening to my son, because he needs to feel heard and understood before coming up with solutions together or by himself. That means working on not being so judgmental, fearful, and worried about his choices.

I have to let him make mistakes because I can't control him, and I shouldn't try to.

Thank you for your amazing advice and support, Cynthia.

Dad Is Determined to Rebuild Relationship with Teen Son

I have a tendency to focus so much on work that I don't spend time with my 16-year-old son. When I do, my relationship with my son improves. When I started working with Cynthia nine months ago, I was focusing on improving my communication and doing activities with my son, and he was opening up to me more.

I've since slipped back into my old habit of putting work first. As a result, my son and I started arguing more. Because of backsliding and not making my son a priority, I haven't been attending our monthly coaching calls with Cynthia as my wife has been. Again, I'm putting work first.

During our most recent coaching call (which I finally attended), Cynthia pointed out that my son will be home for only 15 more months before he leaves for college. This is my last chance to build the connection with him that I truly want.

Since that call, I've made a new determination to go out with my son once a month, no matter what. I know my wife appreciates Cynthia getting through to me about how important my son is to me. Sometimes, it's easier to listen to an "expert" than to my wife.

Mom Learns How to Encourage Her Teenager

My daughter struggles with school and taking initiative. She gets discouraged easily, and recently, she was complaining about a teacher. I've been working with Cynthia to become a better parent so that my kids will do things without being told or after being told only once.

I received a text from my 17-year-old daughter saying, "Get me out of here! My teacher totally overestimates me. She's driving me crazy."

So, I responded with advice to help her solve the problem, "Go find your counselor. See what's going on. See if you can have a conversation with her."

My daughter's complaining continued, "She accused me of being untrustworthy, and I'm innocent." I continued with questioning, giving advice, and sarcasm, "Did you explain? Go talk to someone. You'll survive." None of these messages made the situation better.

Luckily, I met with Cynthia right after this exchange. Cynthia taught me how to respond so that I could be the support my daughter needed to solve her own struggles. This would build her self-confidence and sense of taking responsibility for herself. Cynthia helped me see that my daughter's school challenges weren't mine to solve.

Going forward, as my daughter continued to share her frustrations, I responded with empathy rather than telling her what to do.

I learned that my daughter needed to vent her emotions so then she could move forward with problem solving on her own. I made empathetic and connecting comments such as, "Hmm, I'm sad that this is so hard for you," and "That sounds frustrating."

As a result, my daughter soon resolved the problem with the teacher on her own and even developed a positive relationship with her. She has also been taking more responsibility around the house.

I realized that by listening with care and without criticism or judgment, my daughter could vent her stuck feelings.

Now, she believes that she can solve her challenges with my support, which has raised her self-esteem. What I thought was helping her grow was actually hindering her maturing. Thank you, Cynthia.

Empathizing Works Better Than Yelling

I have an 11-year-old son who struggles with school. We enrolled him in a private school, and he agreed to do the work, but the homework at his new school is turning out to be very challenging. I've gotten mad at him many times when he lies about completing his work, because either he wasn't living up to his end of the bargain, or he just won't do the work to the best of his ability. Whenever I get mad, it only makes matters worse. He gets angry back at me, and it takes a long time for him to calm down and do his homework.

My wife and I went to Cynthia for help with this problem. I was looking at my son as the source of the problem who needed to change. Cynthia taught us to approach the problem by thinking about what we can think, feel, and do differently to bring out a better reaction from our son.

Recently, my son got a poor grade on a test. I felt angry inside, and I wanted to yell at him and say things like, "Why didn't you study more? I pay all this good money for your school, and you don't even try." Instead, I contained my anger, sat down next to my son, and worked on empathizing with him. I said, "You must feel bad about getting this poor grade." (Cynthia teaches us to not say "must," but I haven't perfected being empathetic, yet.) Then, I made some more empathetic statements and was shocked when my son said that he was angry about how he did on the test. He actually opened up about his feelings rather than being hurt by my yelling and yelling back.

I felt great about controlling myself. My son completed his homework much earlier in the evening than he would have if I had yelled. We are also working on having problem-solving discussions about many other challenges such as our two sons fighting in the car. My wife and I will continue to work with Cynthia because we're learning a new parenting approach that makes everyone happier and works much better than yelling and threats.

Thank you, Cynthia.

Dad Listens and Stops Trying to "Fix" His Teenage Daughter

I have a 15-year-old daughter who gets mad at me when I try to help her. Through working with Cynthia, I discovered that what I thought was "help" wasn't helpful. I picked my daughter up from school one day, and she was very upset because she wasn't able to finish her chemistry homework, despite the help of her tutor. This is how our interaction would've gone before I learned better communication skills from Cynthia.

> **Daughter:** "I didn't even finish my chemistry homework with the tutor, and I won't be able to finish by myself. I'm not doing well at all."

> **Me:** "You could get more help from your tutor."

> **Daughter:** "That's not going to help at all. I'm just stupid. Life is horrible. You're no help."

> **Me:** "No, you're very smart. This is just a hard class, and you should go see the teacher again."

> **Daughter:** "You don't understand."

These kinds of interactions always ended with my daughter upset with me. I felt bad that she was struggling, and I felt partially responsible for her problems, so I thought I needed to fix things. After meeting with Cynthia once, I learned that all my daughter needs from me is for me to be a good listener. She needs to vent her feelings, and I need to work on not feeling so responsible for her pain. This is how my interaction with my daughter actually went when I didn't tell her what to do.

Daughter: "I didn't even finish my chemistry homework with the tutor, and I won't be able to finish by myself. I'm not doing well at all."

Me: Silence. I said nothing.

Daughter: "It just doesn't matter. Now I don't have enough time to get ready for diving."

Me: Silence

Daughter: "I'm not going to pass the test, I can't do the homework, and I don't have the time or ability to even do the homework."

The entire time I said nothing because the first step I learned from Cynthia was to avoid blocking communication. Next, I'll be working on how to respond with empathy so that my daughter feels more connected to me. During the interaction referenced above, my daughter never got angry at me. When we got home, she shared more with her mom, and then she was ok. What a difference listening made!

Getting over the feeling that I need to say something to "fix" things has helped me avoid escalating situations. It's great to know that one change can have such a tremendous positive impact on my communication and connection with my daughter. I look forward to learning more from Cynthia.

Connecting with Kids Is the Key to Creating Change

Through working with Cynthia privately, I've discovered that creating a stronger connection with my kids is the foundation for all positive change within the family. I'm divorced with a 10-year-old daughter and a 12-year-old son. There is conflict with their father, which makes discipline more difficult.

I had developed a habit of giving in to my son's demands because he would yell if I didn't. This pattern started when he was young, and I didn't know what to do to change it. I would resort to saying, "You have to..." and "You should..." as a means of trying to get him to obey. This approach didn't work and led to more conflict and resistance.

I'll admit that I'm struggling with making changes. I often forget and resort back to my old patterns. I'm improving, though, on giving directions, like putting away clothes, and making sure that my son follows through, no matter what it takes. Cynthia has given me the courage and skills to persevere.

What I have learned and am working on consistently is how to create greater connections with my son. Every day, I make time to talk with him. It's easier to spend time with my daughter and more challenging to connect with a 12-year-old boy.

My son likes to talk about computers, science, and health. I recently purchased a DVD of the TV show, *House, M.D.*, which he likes, and we watch it together. This shared time makes us feel closer, and as a result, my son is more responsive when I ask him for help around the house. I plan to keep focusing on finding ways to connect with my son on a daily basis. I know that I need to change more in order to parent better. I will continue to engage in self-reflection and work on implementing Cynthia's ideas, one step at a time. Each of my small changes brings about a positive change in the family.

Morning Goes Well When Parent Connects with Child

Hi, Cynthia.

I attended your recent talk on how to encourage your kids to do what you need them to do and tried out your suggestions today. I spent six minutes of quality time with my older son this morning, doing what he wanted to do, and it was amazing how that quality time transformed him. He did all his chores, ate breakfast, brushed his teeth, and got his bag ready for school. It was like a miracle! I know that this is a work in progress, but it was the first time in I don't know how long that he didn't cry.

Thank you so much for your guidance!

No Longer Anxious Parents

We started private coaching with Cynthia during the spring of our son's sophomore year of high school. We were concerned that he wasn't doing his homework the best that he could. We kept trying to give him advice, but he would always get angry with us, telling us to leave him alone. We wanted him to earn straight A grades, but he would always get one B.

Through a series of questions from Cynthia, we gained insight into our anxiety and need to pressure our son so much. Now, we're more able to let it go. We grew up in another country where it was very difficult, and doing well in school was the only way to change one's situation. We kept seeing our son as not doing enough because he wasn't handling school and studying the same way we did as teens.

The root of the problem was our anxiety, not the fact that our son wasn't studying the way we wanted him to. Below is a summary of a very important conversation that helped us understand ourselves and our son better so that we could change our beliefs.

Anxious Parents: "We keep giving him advice because we just want our son to be better than us."

Cynthia: "Why do you want him to be better than you? You are not good enough? Do you think making him better than you will make him happier? You are not happy?"

Anxious Parents: "I'm good, I'm proud of myself, and I'm happy."

Cynthia: "Will you be happy if your son is like you? Why do you want him to be better than you?"

Anxious Parents: "Yes, but we still want him to be better than us because he has much better conditions than us."

Cynthia: "Better conditions doesn't mean he'll be a better person. Being a better person comes from hardship. Because you struggled as you did, you became the people you are now."

Anxious Parents: "Yes, you're right! We never thought of it that way. Thank you!"

Our son is now a junior in high school, and our relationship has improved so much because of our more relaxed and trusting approach with him. He's doing very well in school, and his desire is coming from within himself. We don't have to push him anymore, and we're so much happier.

Section 3

Understanding Yourself and Your Child

14.
The Key to Making Positive Parenting Changes Stick

As children grow older, they want and need to become more independent. Children's increasing need for independence is challenging for parents because it often means that they don't want to be told what to do. This separation process can lead to more conflicts and power struggles. It is important to evaluate your current parenting approach and decide whether it will continue to be effective as your children mature. If not, you can start making parenting changes now.

Chances are you've read numerous parenting books and attended parenting classes to find answers to your parent-child challenges. If you've tried the proposed solutions, such as ways to control your anger, you may be having difficulty making your desired parenting changes stick. The ideas sound good, and you follow through for a while, but then your old habits take over again, and you feel discouraged.

The key to more permanent behavior changes is that your beliefs are consistent with your actions. When you focus only on changing your actions without learning the complementary beliefs that underlie those actions, your success will be minimal. To make changes stick, you must first understand the underlying beliefs and attitudes behind your ineffective actions. Then, you can learn the beliefs and attitudes that match your new desired actions.

The Think-Feel-Do Cycle teaches us that what we think triggers how we feel, and how we feel influences our actions. Your child's Think-Feel-Do Cycle operates in tandem with your side of the Think-Feel-Do Cycle. You can respond to their actions reactively, and they can then respond to you reactively. This can create a vicious cycle in which you give up your personal power and instead feel controlled by your children. You can regain your power by breaking the chain of reactivity through making positive changes to the "thinking" part of your cycle first. This, in turn, brings about more positive changes in your children.

A common misconception about changing kids' behavior is that parents have to directly change what their child does. You can experience how ineffective this is when you loudly command, "Stop hitting your sister!" "Turn off the TV!" and "It's time to go to bed!" with no compliance. In response to your attempts at overt parental control, your child becomes an immovable object.

Here are some common parental beliefs behind these types of commanding statements. These beliefs are often learned in childhood.

- *Parents are right because they are the adults, and children need to learn how to follow rules. Whether parents and children feel connected isn't as important.*

- *Children act badly because they're trying to get back at or manipulate their parents.*

- *My children need to live up to my expectations of them without questioning or disagreeing with me. My goals are more important than theirs.*

- *When children start to get out of control, I need to control them.*

You can choose alternative discipline approaches to create more cooperation with children. These alternatives include the After-Then Strategy, listening to emotions and stating expectations clearly, and problem solving together. To implement these approaches, you must shift from believing you need to control children to believing you can guide children by working together with them.

Here are the beliefs and attitudes that match the positive parenting approaches listed above.

- *My parenting actions are based on the belief that I am emotionally and physically available for my child as much as possible.*

- *My child is her/his own person, and it is not for me to mold her/him to my own expectations. I will hold my judgment and criticism in check when they are hurtful.*

- *The relationship between me and my child is more important than being right all the time.*

Children's basic nature is to love their parents. A feeling of disconnection from others can lead to misbehavior and poor thinking. Try to view your children's misbehavior from their perspective to help them meet their needs positively.

Take time to write down all the thoughts you're having about your child and yourself during recurring conflicts. Are your beliefs creating the relationship you want? Which ones are you willing to discard? Then, explore new beliefs that will support your new actions. You may benefit from private parenting coaching through this process.

Practice stating your new beliefs aloud before the conflict occurs again. At the start of the conflict, stop yourself and repeat those beliefs silently to yourself. With your new beliefs, the effective, connecting actions will come more often. When you falter, simply try again. With renewed determination, you will gradually make your positive parenting thoughts and changes stick, resulting in greater happiness for yourself and your family.

15.
Problem Solving Together Requires Flexible Thinking

Imagine you are having a conflict with your child because he won't do his homework. You're in a deadlock because you are determined to change your child, and your child is determined to resist your pushing. Behind your determination are beliefs that it is his homework and he needs to be responsible for getting it done. You are also thinking that you shouldn't have to nag him and that he could do it if he would only try harder. Because of your inflexible and judgmental perspective, your child builds walls and barriers to any possibility of solving problems together.

Mary and Bob held a "we're right and you're wrong" adversarial position with their daughter who struggled with homework. They judged her with questions and statements like, "Why won't you let us help you?" "You could do it if you didn't spend so much time talking with your friends," and "You say you want better grades, but then you don't try harder." Their unhelpful attempts at advising, criticizing, blaming, and shaming her into being "responsible" caused her to pull away and not accept their help.

Mary and Bob needed a more flexible Ally perspective. Only then could they create an environment in which everyone would listen to each other and share responsibility for solving the homework dilemma. By bringing an Ally perspective, their daughter would be more willing to discuss her challenges with her parents and find helpful solutions.

In order to break through the parent-child power struggle deadlock, children need parents who increase their flexible beliefs and actions while minimizing their inflexible beliefs and actions. In order to make this shift, there are three key steps you should follow.

First, eliminate all judgmental thoughts and statements containing words such as "should have," "could have," "shouldn't," "but," and "if only."

These words hurt because they disregard the child's feelings and perspective, leading to emotional shutdown, rebellion, or revenge. Next, clearly state the facts of the situation, as you see them, without judgment. Finally, discuss problem-solving solutions based on reality, if possible, rather than your expectations and fears.

Mary and Bob realized that they needed to transform some deep-rooted inflexible beliefs influenced by their own childhood experiences and triggered by adult fears. They were afraid that their daughter wouldn't succeed in school or attend college, thereby reducing her earning potential. Their projected fears caused them to be adversaries rather than allies, so they were not able to help their daughter. Rather than staying stuck in fear, they gradually learned how to remain in the moment by choosing new, flexible thoughts. As a result, they discussed and resolved problems together with compassionate support.

When Mary and Bob empathized with their daughter and shifted from being adversaries to allies, the wall came down. They discovered that she didn't understand her math homework. She now accepts her mom's help and understands her assignments. Her grades have gone from failing to great!

Mary and Bob learned how to use this conflict-turned-deadlock situation to better understand themselves and their daughter. Through this process, they developed inner strength, courage, and confidence as an ally with influence rather than an adversary without authority.

When you learn how to think flexibly, you parent with compassion, wisdom, and expertise. Any time you feel stuck, step back from the situation and take a moment for self-reflection. Engage in the following self-dialogue: *How am I adversarial? How do I create and prolong the current conflict? I must let go of my righteous beliefs and instead listen to my child with an open mind and heart as an ally would. With this approach, I know my family will build bridges to understanding and roads to happy and successful lives.*

Refer to the chart on the next page to learn how to shift from inflexible thinking to flexible thinking.

Old judgmental, inflexible thinking:	New Ally, flexible thinking:
If she would only try harder, she would finish.	Even though she wants to complete the homework, she can't. She really doesn't understand it and needs help.
If she didn't rush through her work, she would do better. Why won't she let us help her?	Maybe she doesn't want help because she's embarrassed that she doesn't understand the work. I've made it difficult for her to share her feelings. This has broken her trust in me.
I shouldn't have to help her so much.	Apparently, she isn't able to do the homework on her own. I need to help her bridge her current limitations and her dreams. I'll tell her I realize it's difficult, and we'll work together to find solutions.

16.
Why Children Do What They Do –
It's Not About You

When your kids don't cooperate with you, it's easy to take their behavior personally, as though they are against you. I call this response the "parent's victim mentality." When you see yourself as a victim, you think your kids are acting against you, that you are the *target* of their behavior. You may think, *They're being disrespectful to me*, or *They're trying to push my buttons*. It becomes all about you rather than what your kids are thinking, feeling, or needing.

This viewpoint often puts your children, not you, in control of your thoughts, feelings, and actions. Here are some common phrases that indicate you're stuck in a parent's victim mentality. "You make me so..." or "If you would just..., then I would..." or even, "I yelled because you..." These beliefs are not effective in building family harmony.

Michael Popkin, PhD, offers a refreshing way to understand children's behavior through understanding the goals behind their behavior. As Dr. Popkin describes it, children are focused on meeting their own needs, or goals, not on going against you. This model allows parents to step out of the stuck victim mentality. When you have a clearer perspective on the reasons for your child's behavior, then you have a greater ability to redirect negative behavior and create positive behavior.

Understanding Behavior - Purpose Not Cause

In order to understand another person's behavior, it's important to understand that humans are beings with free will who choose how to behave based on their experience, values, and goals for the future. So, instead of asking your child, "Why did you do that?" ask yourself, *What is their goal? What is the "payoff" their behavior is aimed at getting?*

Children have four goals, while teenagers and adults have an additional fifth goal. The child's four goals are Belonging, Power, Protection, and Withdrawal. The additional teenage/adult goal is Challenge.

Belonging

The basic need of every human being is to belong. Belonging is critical for our survival. Driven by this desire to belong, each of us develops the goal of making contact – physical or emotional – with other human beings. Contact with parents or primary caregivers helps the growing child develop a sense of belonging within the family. As teenagers begin to look toward the future, they feel a stronger need to create connection with friends and other groups outside the family.

Power

Each of us wants to influence our environment and gain at least a measure of control over it. As parents, our challenge is to guide and protect children, while at the same time increasing the amount of power and control they have over their lives. This is a gradual transition from dependence to independence.

Protection

All people have a desire to protect themselves, both physically and emotionally. Your child's need to protect their personal identity becomes a driving force during their teenage years, which explains why teenagers become angry when they're restricted. Some teenagers will do whatever they need to have their goals met. This includes lying to you. Be careful to not become the victim and view their lying as being disrespectful to you. Rather, see it as a means for them to get what they want.

Withdrawal

The development of one's own identity leads most children to withdraw into their own space. They need time and privacy to sort out changes and understand their new world and their place in it. There are two exceptions to giving children privacy: if you suspect drug or alcohol use and if your child is depressed.

Challenge - Begins during the teen years

The desire to test skill and courage against an obstacle is one way teenagers measure how well they're doing on their journey from dependence to independence. This is a natural part of growing up. Many teenagers create their own challenges by challenging you.

Each of the five goals can be met through behavior that is either negative or positive. Listed in the following chart are the five goals, negative and positive actions to achieve each goal, and your possible emotional reactions. Use your feelings during your child's negative behavior to help you determine your child's goal.

Child's Goal	Positive Approach	Negative Approach	Your Feelings Toward Your Child/Teen
Belonging	Contributing, Cooperating	Undue Attention Seeking	Annoyance
Power	Independence	Rebellion	Anger
Protection	Assertiveness, Forgiveness	Revenge	Hurt
Withdrawal	Appropriate Avoidance	Undue Avoidance	Helplessness
Challenge (Teens & Adults only)	Safe Adventures	Thrill Seeking	Fear

When you discover your children's goals, rather than feel helpless and confused, you can offer opportunities for them to meet those goals positively. Because they have learned negative patterns with you, you have the power to turn the tide and guide them towards positive patterns with you. This is why I keep stressing that you are the one who can change the situation, not your child. They will change in response to your changes. How exciting!

If you are annoyed, chances are that your child is trying to belong and they are doing it in an irritating way. To steer her in a positive direction, give her undivided attention regularly before the misbehavior begins so you build a sense of connection and security within her. Instead of nagging and coaxing, stop what you are doing and give your child full attention without using communication blocks. See if they need help with a task. Make sure your expectations are reasonable. If possible, be there as emotional support if they need to cry, talk, and/or tremble or shake to release tension so they can think clearly and make better decisions. Think of ways she can contribute positively.

If you feel angry, chances are your child is rebelling against you because they want power and you are taking it away. Rather than continuing the power struggle, check to see if you are directing and taking away power when instead you could collaborate or support, which gives power. Your child will learn positive ways for power when you have family meetings for group decision making or confidently support their own decisions.

If you feel hurt by your child, he is probably trying to protect himself through hurting you back with revenge. Telling him that you are hurt focuses on you, rather than your child's hurt, and it doesn't teach him how to assertively express himself. So, instead of telling him to stop, think, *I have hurt my child and he is hurting me back. It's best to listen with empathy and allow my child to be assertive and tell me, "Dad, I don't like it when you won't let me have dessert first."* This will teach him to self-reflect and tell you what he is really thinking rather than attacking you.

If you feel helpless, your child's goal is probably negative withdrawal by avoiding challenges. This can happen when children struggle academically. They lose confidence in their ability to succeed and parents can lose confidence as well. Instead, tell him that whether he succeeds or fails, your love is unconditional. As you practice patience and encouragement, help her find tasks that she can perform successfully to begin to break the misconception of herself as a loser. Also, create a family atmosphere where mistakes are for learning and failure is just a lesson on the road to success. These are important values as you solve problems together without harsh judgment or criticism.

You'll know your teen is using thrill-seeking to feel challenged if you're unusually afraid for your daughter or son. An additional sign is when she misbehaves and if, when you discipline her, she responds by taking even more reckless risks. When you try to stifle her need to test herself or to discover her identity, thrill-seeking often becomes stronger. If you react with anger and outrage when your teen drinks or engages in other harmful thrill-seeking behavior, the teen now has two motivations to continue; the thrill itself and to show Mom and Dad they can't run her life.

Avoid power struggles by remaining firm and calm. Encourage him to find a source of income such as babysitting or taking care of other's pets. Redirect your teen toward positive activities such as karate, cycling, rock climbing, white-water sports, team sports, or a dance group. Enjoy vicarious thrills by going to sporting events. Spend meaningful time by learning something together. Respect your teen and let him know he is important in society because he is our future decision maker.

Realize that events outside of your control, such as hardships at school and with friends, can lead to poor self-esteem and then to risky behavior. During this difficult time, it's important to support and believe in his potential even when it's not being manifested. Your belief will help him believe in himself.

17.
The Strong-Willed Child's Attitudes and Power Struggle Triggers

Most parents of strong-willed children find them to be very challenging. Parents have conflicting desires between wanting easy-going children, so that they will do what they're told, and also wanting strong-willed kids, so that they will stand up for themselves and not be swayed by negative influences. Since this dual personality doesn't exist, it's best to first learn how strong-willed children think and how your language could be triggering additional power struggles with them.

Strong-willed children respond best to Director parents who state expectations clearly and with a strong, doubt-free, and loving voice. With strong-willed children, it's best to maintain this same demeanor even if you aren't sure what to say in the moment by responding, "I need to think more, and then I will give you my answer." Then, be sure to stop responding.

Here are some strong-willed beliefs and attitudes that may be at the core of your children's dominant actions. You may see yourself in these beliefs and attitudes, as well. Which ones do you think your child believes?

- *I deserve to be treated fairly and justly.*

- *I believe that my thoughts and feelings are as important as yours.*

- *I may push loudly to be heard because I fear that my needs will be ignored.*

- *I will insist on having power over my life.*

- *I may not feel comfortable being gentle or giving, for these attitudes seem "soft" or "weak" to me.*

- *The more I feel rejected, betrayed, or in pain, the more I put up my guard.*

- *I may make it hard for you to show me warmth and love because I may not respond in kind (even though I need your love and feel love myself).*

- *Just because you are my parent, that doesn't mean you're right or that you can treat me disrespectfully.*

- *My tendency is to be interested in getting what I want before you get what you want.*

- *I respond well to honesty, straightforwardness, and trust.*

- *I do not respond well to threats, use of force, or any other methods of control. When faced with attempts to control me, I will likely stand up for myself by rebelling against you.*

- *I may have a hard time asking for support or help because I'm afraid that I'll lose my autonomy.*

- *I am happiest when you allow me to be independent.*

- *I may be very territorial about my things. I don't want anyone to touch them. This helps me feel safe.*

- *I may be stubborn, impassive, and quietly menacing.*

- *When I lose my temper, the explosion comes suddenly, violently, and then it's gone.*

To win cooperation from strong-willed children, focus on not being adversarial, pleading, or fearful of resistance. These types of responses feel disrespectful or weak to the strong-willed child, which will diminish your authority and often open the door to power struggles. Avoid these common responses and replace with effective directives:

- Answering your kid's "Why?" questions when they already know the answer. You'll end up defending yourself and trying to convince them to change their resistance. You don't need their agreement in order for them to comply.

- Asking "Will you, please?" when it isn't a choice.

- Stating your request based on your needs, such as "I want you to" and "I need you to." These can trigger power struggles because your needs are more important than the needs of the situation.

- Adding "Okay?" at the end of your directions to try to gain their approval.

- Giving a "consequence" that feels like a punishment to teach your kids "a lesson."

- Counting "1...2...3" aloud as a means to scare your children into doing what you want. Most parents don't know what to do if they get past "3."

- Shaming your children with statements such as, "How many times do I have to tell you?" "Why did you do that?" "You should've known better," and "You're a bad boy/girl."

- Making threats like, "If you don't do (what I want), then (something bad) will happen."

- Using exaggerations, including "never," "always," "everybody," "nobody," "every time," and "all the time."

- Commanding with, "you should," "you'd better," "you ought to," "you can't," and "you will." These are instant power struggle trigger phrases and lead to your child trying to gain power through rebellion.

- Talking too much and making your directions longer rather than shorter.

- Assuming your kids should act like adults or blaming them when thinking:

o   *I shouldn't have to say it more than once.*

o   *They should know better.*

o   *I already told him how to (clean his room, do his laundry, dust, etc.).*

o   *I'm so tired of repeating myself.*

Both strong-willed parents and conflict-avoiding parents experience challenges in learning how to respond effectively. Start by eliminating a few of your problem phrases, like making threats. Just one small change on your part will greatly increase your influence and result in many positive changes in your kids.

18.
How to Melt the Walls Between Mothers and Daughters

The mother-daughter relationship is particularly challenging because both sides desire and value emotional connection, whether it's negative or positive. Because of this deep desire, when circumstances erode the emotional connection, both parties feel hurt and can resort to unhelpful language and actions that further the divide. However, even after a wall has developed, I have guided many mothers with daughters ages 8 to 18 through the process of melting the wall. The length of time required to melt the wall depends on how deep the divide between mother and daughter has become. The good news is that your perseverance can create a reconnection.

Some walls are thin. With these walls, as soon as you start the reconnection process, which I will discuss below, you can melt the barrier quickly. As your daughter opens up, reconnection is gained. Other walls are thick due to your daughter feeling hurt and protecting herself repeatedly over several years. Special challenges, such as sensory integration, anxiety, inattention, or impulse control, make walls especially difficult to melt. It's normal for you to feel frustrated on a daily basis, and that frustration can cause hurtful words and actions by both of you. Even a thick wall of mutual hurt and lack of trust can melt, though, when you learn the reconnection process.

The reconnection process starts with you taking full responsibility for discovering which of your past actions have hurt your daughter and then taking steps to melt the wall. If you keep waiting for your daughter to change first, you will be powerless, frustrated, and discouraged. The full responsibility approach gives you the power to improve your relationship.

As soon as you think, *Okay, I'm going to make our relationship better,* it's time to be vulnerable with your daughter and discuss communication blocks. This is the scary part of the process because what if you admit that you've been blocking communication and she uses it against you? Even though every mother fears this response, I have never heard of a daughter turning on her mother in this way. Your vulnerability starts to warm your daughter's heart toward you, even if this isn't outwardly apparent right away. Although she won't turn on you, your daughter's response will range from talking openly about the communication blocks to getting upset and refusing to talk with you about it.

If your daughter refuses to talk with you because she feels deeply hurt, trust is broken, and she isn't ready to forgive you yet, don't despair. In fact, expect her wall to remain in place for a while as you become vulnerable and she learns to trust you again. As you work on being vulnerable, which can include writing a letter to her and not blocking communication, also make sure to use the appropriate parenting role - Director, Collaborator, or Supporter/Confidant - for each situation. You have likely used an incorrect parenting role in the past, such as being a Director rather than a Collaborator, which has contributed to your daughter putting up a protective wall. In summary, the reconnection process requires taking full responsibility, being vulnerable as you discuss your communication blocks, and choosing the appropriate parenting role for each situation.

Even if you feel that there's no way to melt the wall, I believe there is because you love your daughter and you are working on improving your relationship. Once you understand how your words have unintentionally hurt her, without feeling guilty, you can choose to change. Your daughter will see this change and start to feel reconnected with you. Your daughter is waiting for you to help her melt the wall and build a bridge so she can cross over to you again.

On one occasion, a mom came to me upset and at her wit's end because her 17-year-old daughter wouldn't speak to her or return her text messages. She felt hopeless, but I knew she could melt the wall between herself and her daughter because she had built it. First, I taught her about avoiding communication blocks and how to listen openly with empathy instead. Through reviewing her communication blocks, the mom realized that she regularly used interrogating, giving advice, and commanding. She was also using the Director Role and taking charge in situations that were her daughter's to decide. Through our work together, she learned how to be a Supporter/Confidant rather than a Director, so her daughter wouldn't have to put up a protective wall to keep her mother out.

The mom talked with her daughter about communication blocks, and her daughter agreed that the mom interrogated, commanded, and gave unwanted advice too much. The mom wanted to change so she worked hard to stop blocking communication and instead listened with empathy when her daughter started trusting her and sharing more. Within a month, her daughter didn't need to keep her mother out by putting up a wall. The daughter trusted her mother so much that she wanted to spend a Friday night with her parents - who were shocked but loved the time they finally had together as a family. In another two weeks, the daughter took her mom to a concert of her choosing, and they had great mother-daughter time together. Because this mom took full responsibility for changing, she created a beautifully connected relationship beyond her wildest dreams.

As you practice the reconnection process, focus on the loving relationship you're determined to create with your daughter, rather than the wall that remains between you. In order to maintain a positive attitude, seek out a support system of people who understand the challenges you're facing and encourage your progress. A loving and connected relationship with your daughter is possible if you learn to take full responsibility, stop blocking communication, and melt away the walls that have been built over time. You will find that those walls come down quicker than they were created.

19.
Supporting the Easily-Distracted Child

Children who are easily distracted, disorganized, and have difficulty prioritizing can drive their parents crazy. Out of frustration, you may resort to judgmental statements that start with:

"Why can't you...?"

"Don't you care about...?"

"If you'd only try harder, you would..."

"When are you going to learn how to be more...?"

"If you made a list, planned ahead, put things back where they belonged, looked more carefully, etc..." (then everything would be just fine, and I wouldn't be so stressed watching you and trying to get you to move.)

Compassion and understanding toward the highly distract-ed child or adult can get lost when faced with time constraints, exhaustion, and unreasonable expectations. I know because I've been married to a highly creative and highly disorganized man for many years, and the story of how I've created a dis-traction-friendly family has been a source of encouragement and wisdom to parents of easily distractible children.

Developing compassion toward the easily-distracted child requires understanding that they are not doing "it" purpose-fully. They know you want them to be responsible, have an organized backpack, and turn their homework in on time. They would love to win your praise.

The first step to creating a distraction-compassionate fam-ily is to understand why you feel so critical of your child. Your judgmental thoughts and statements could be traced back to personal and/or cultural beliefs, such as:

- *Willpower and hard work will get you through anything.*

- *Cleanliness is next to godliness.*

- *Don't start something you're not willing to finish.*

- *There's a right way and a wrong way to do things.*

Ask yourself whether you're willing to let go of beliefs that are damaging your relationship with your child. Can you love your child for their amazing qualities and kindly accept their challenges? Every day, I appreciate what my husband brings to our relationship. Then, I accept and embrace my role as the main organizer in the family.

The second step to creating a distraction-compassionate family is to understand the inner confusion and disorganization in your child's mind. Rather than a deficit of attention, your child may have difficulty utilizing attention, directing it, putting it in the right place at the right time as they wish. Often, it means that they just can't think of what to do. Some kids can't think of an idea and act on it. They become paralyzed and getting upset with them doesn't help the situation. A common example of this phenomenon is when your child won't clean their room because they don't know where to start.

For many easily-distracted children, trying to find ideas for a particular purpose inside their head can be as difficult as finding papers on a messy desk. It is hard for many distracted, creative kids to pull all their ideas together, whether verbally or in writing. An overabundance of ideas can overwhelm and lead to difficulty organizing those ideas. The easily-distracted child can freeze up and say, "I don't know," or take a long time to respond as they figure out what they're actually thinking and what to say. When faced with these challenges, you need great patience.

As soon as you understand your own emotional triggers and how your child's overabundance of ideas interferes with focus, you'll be ready for the third step, creating a distraction-friendly home.

The goal is to create a home environment in which family members:

- Seek out ways to simplify routines and solve problems

- Are supportive, loving, and cooperative

- Don't "sweat the details" or hyperfocus on mistakes

- Learn to laugh about distraction, emphasizing what family members do right

- Believe it's okay to be different from one another and to be oneself

- Spend time enjoying each other, not focusing only on problems

Creating a distraction-friendly home doesn't mean that you make sure everything is done right. Be careful of resentment building up because you do too much to make up for other family members' disorganization. To avoid this pitfall, set boundaries around what you will and won't do and stick to them.

To support your easily-distracted child, teach them that their inner turmoil can be managed and solutions can be found. You want them to learn coping skills for a successful life. Try saying, "I realize your brain is so full of ideas that it's hard to focus. You'll always have many thoughts in your head that can feel overwhelming. Let's work together to help you manage your thoughts and feel good about yourself." Your child's success begins with you believing in them, valuing their uniqueness, working on reducing your judgmental thoughts, and focusing on their good qualities instead.

Section 4

The Director Role – Setting Limits and Boundaries

20.
Choose the Discipline Path for Family Harmony

Parents desire loving relationships with their children so that their children will trust them and seek them out for support and advice. Throughout many years of teaching parenting classes, it has become clear to me that well-meaning parents are resorting to ineffective punishment strategies, strategies that hurt the parent-child relationship, because they simply don't know what else to do.

Parents are unhappy with the lack of cooperation and respect they're receiving from their kids. They're also unhappy with their own lack of emotional control and how they're treating their children. Under duress, they quickly resort to using the same negative parenting tactics they experienced as children. This approach is working against their desire to create a supportive and harmonious family where children develop their talents, are valued, and contribute their opinions.

Parents report using "consequences" or threats such as, "If you don't pick up your toys right now, you won't play your video game." Imagine how you felt as a child hearing this type of threat. As an adult, you may think that this sounds like a logical consequence, yet the tone, word usage, and word placement communicate a threat. As a result, parents report being mocked, ignored, or even laughed at by their children with comments like, "You're not going to take it away."

Parents are stunned and embarrassed when their kids sound just like them. In one of my parenting classes, a mother recounted how her son threatened her with, "If you don't let me play, then I won't brush my teeth." Threats that once put fear into these parents as kids do not create the close relationships that the parents in my classes want with their children.

In an attempt to be nicer than their parents were, parents begin with "nicer" controlling strategies, such as asking politely, explaining their reasoning to win agreement, and giving rewards. Although "nicer," this approach still doesn't work with children. When these "gentler" attempts fail to elicit positive responses, parents resort to unsuccessful punishment strategies, such as instilling guilt, pleading, yelling, and threatening.

The bottom line is that taking an obedience strategy based on manipulation and instilling fear and then expecting cooperation, respect, and responsibility in return doesn't work. This approach isn't logical. In order to create a successful family, punishment strategies must be avoided and replaced with discipline methods that teach important life skills.

The following parenting strategies are focused on controlling children to gain compliance. In response to these controlling strategies, children learn, either directly or indirectly, that they are a bad person. While regretting poor choices upon self-reflection is a desirable outcome, a child thinking of himself as a bad person is detrimental to making better choices in the future. Avoid the following authoritarian punishment strategies:

- Isolating and blaming children when they're upset as a means to teach them that emotional outbursts are unacceptable

- Using shaming and judgmental language to belittle, such as "You should have..." or "You're so stupid, careless, etc."

- Creating rewards and bribes to control behavior

- Designing a contrived consequence that feels unfair, which creates a barrier of anger and resentment against the adult rather than self-reflection on the part of the child

- Ignoring, discounting, or ridiculing your children's thoughts and feelings

- Yelling to gain compliance

For parents who want to break this cycle of authoritarian power over children, I recommend using an Ally discipline parenting approach. Announce your new approach to your children as you gradually replace old punishment strategies with new discipline teaching strategies.

Here are some examples of how to guide and teach children:

- Take responsibility for the impact of your behavior by choosing your actions with this question in mind, *Is what I'm about to say or do going to build up or break down the parent-child relationship? Because, ultimately, that's all that matters.*

- Listen openly with curiosity about your children's thoughts and feelings so they can get unstuck, build trust with you, and feel safe.

- Use respectful directives, such as "After you (work), then you can (play)" or "It's time to (work)."

- Solve problems together so children can learn how to think logically and creatively.

- Set clear negotiable and non-negotiable rules that shift as your children mature.

- Seek out your own emotional support so you can parent from wisdom rather than fear.

If your goal is to create a family that sticks together through thick and thin, then learn more about the benefits of my Ally discipline approach. A good first step is to use the After-Then Strategy as an effective directive to gain cooperation rather than commanding, asking, or threatening. Learn how to effectively apply this approach in Chapter 23, *Director Parenting Role: The After-Then Strategy*, in Section 4.

21.
Give Directions Kids Will Follow

Your goal in the Director Parenting Role is to teach your children to become responsible and capable by learning important life skills, such as cleaning up after themselves, using respectful language, making commitments and sticking to them, getting along with others, and following rules set by authority. I encourage discussing these important values with your children while keeping in mind that they may not embrace your values right away.

If you are having difficulty getting your kids to respond to your directions, you are probably too commanding, too pleasing, or a combination of both. A minor shift in your language may be all you need to improve your children's positive response rate.

Commanding language tells kids that they need to do what you want them to do. This approach feels like a challenge to a strong-willed child and can lead to defiance. Provoking statements often start with, "I want you to...," "You need to...," and "You're supposed to..."

Just as ineffective as commanding statements are attempts to soften a potential emotional outburst from your children by adding "please," "okay," and "would you" to your directions. You may use these "softening" words because you want your children to feel they have some power in the decision-making process or because you think this is the respectful way to act. However, when you are directing, you are not solving problems together. Respect toward your child is best expressed through your caring tone of voice and respectful demeanor, not "pleasing" words.

The problem is that "pleasing" words like those listed above turn your directions into requests that can be easily ignored. You do not need your child's approval. Rather, your goal is to get acknowledgment and agreement that they have heard you and will cooperate with you.

Here are some examples of directives that are weakened with "okay," "please," or "would you":

"You need to turn off the TV now, okay?"

"Would you please put your toys away?"

"I want you to eat your dinner before you have dessert, okay?"

"Please clean the bathroom before you go to your friend's house."

"You can be on the computer for 30 minutes, okay?"

Bear in mind that children respond best to effective directives when they feel emotionally connected to you. Make sure you are spending time listening to your kids and playing with them. If they are having a hard time responding to you, learn how to be a more effective listener. Read other articles to learn this important communication skill. Remember that as a parent, you create change in your kids through connection and influence, not control.

One effective Director strategy is the "Just-the-Facts" approach. You are not asking, pleading, or trying to please in order to get your needs met. You are simply stating the expectation in a calm and direct manner. This eliminates the opportunity for your child to use arguing and tantrums to manipulate you. Avoid getting mad at your kids if they complain. That's their job. Your Director Role is to set up structure so they can successfully learn the life skills you are trying to teach them.

It's important to give directions with total confidence that your respectful and reasonable directive will be followed. Remember that when you change how you interact with your kids, you will bring out a more positive response from them. You will be amazed by how cooperative your kids will be when you speak to them with respectful authority.

Here are some examples of the "Just-the-Facts" approach:

"It's time to turn off the TV."

"Toys need to be put away now."

"You can be on the computer for 30 minutes. Do you understand?"

Do not yell or sound irritated when you have to repeat your directive. Also, don't respond with, "How many times do I have to tell you?" If they complain, ask why, or try to argue, do not engage. Parents get trapped into thinking they need to answer "why" whenever it is asked because they think it's rude not to. If your kids know why, calmly and respectfully shorten your directions and repeat the expectation.

If you are giving directions with confidence, without commanding or pleading, repeating the directive three times should be enough at first. Soon, repeating only once will be sufficient. This approach is particularly effective with teenagers who love to argue. Saying fewer words is better than explaining yourself.

"TV off."

"Toys away."

"30 minutes, only."

An additional strategy that parents find helpful in setting time limits on electronics is the Time-Limit Strategy. For this process to be effective, you'll need a timer and a willingness to follow through. As with all Director Role strategies, you must first build a solid connection with your child through empathetic listening and problem solving together, at another time, in order for your child to be responsive to you. Setting the time limit before your child begins to use their electronic device is preferable, but if you forget to set the limit in advance, you can still use this approach.

Step 1: Establish eye contact with your child. This is crucial. Do not allow yourself to be ignored. You could say, "It's important that I know you're listening to me right now. Looking at me helps me know."

Step 2: State the limit clearly. "You can use the tablet for one hour."

Step 3: Get acknowledgment from your child that you were heard. "What did I say?"

Step 4: Get agreement from your child. "And you understand that the tablet will be handed to me in one hour? I'll give you a 10-minute warning, and no more time after that." (You are continuing to maintain eye contact, or close to it, while you say this. Otherwise, your child cannot use the device. You do not accept, "Okay, okay," as they are doing something else. If they do, say, "In order to play, you must pay attention to me now.")

Step 5: Give a 10-minute warning to help your child prepare for stopping the activity. "You have 10 more minutes, and then you must stop."

Step 6: Enforce the limit. "Time's up." Then, collect the device.

Step 7: Thank your child for cooperating. "Thank you for getting off on time." Some children respond better when you add an empathetic statement, such as, "It's difficult to stop when you're having fun. I appreciate your cooperation. It makes it easier to give you the tablet again the next time you ask for it."

You may be thinking, *I've tried this*, or, *What happens if they don't give me the device? Do I grab it?* Don't engage in a tug-of-war. This will only make matters worse and can end up with you being physical and your child responding in kind. By the time you feel like grabbing the device, you can't think logically because you are so angry or frustrated. You may be thinking, *My child is so disobedient, I'm the parent and she needs to listen to me, He has got to get to bed* or even, *I do so much for him and this is how he treats me.* If you get to this point, stop yourself and say, "I'm going away for five minutes then I will be back for the computer." Then leave and calm yourself down. Don't say anything about their behavior, rather state the expectation of what will happen in five minutes. Then try again.

It's very important to work on building connection even before you start setting limits where you have been lax before. Parents often don't want to do the emotional connecting part because they think kids should just listen and do what they are told. This is adversarial thinking and probably the reason you haven't been successful in setting limits in the past. You have to discard these beliefs and embrace Ally beliefs instead. Many parents have reported to me that when they spend time connecting with their children through listening, the Time-Limit Strategy is effective. I'm not saying to listen during the limit setting. Rather, spend time listening without blocking communication when you pick them up from school, when they seem frustrated from homework, and when they want to share what happened during the day.

If you experience good conversations and there is still angry resistance to stopping, then you have a bigger problem. Your child may be unable to stop himself due to the positive stimulation of video games. I suggest getting professional help because you need personal guidance on how to restrict electronics use.

Generally, the more you are clear with your limits and expectations without getting upset or giving in to their attempts at negotiating for more, the more they will respect your limits. Deep inside they actually appreciate your clarity and firmness. Everyone will feel happier when you aren't nagging your kids and they know you won't be swayed by them. Whew! What a relief!

22.
Add Connecting to Improve Directing

For Director parenting strategies to work, children need to feel connected to the adult giving a directive. It isn't enough for you to just learn, for example, the After-Then Strategy, to win cooperation. There needs to be a balance in your parent-child relationships between nurturing through listening and problem solving and structuring through setting limits.

There are many situations where parents need to set parameters in order to get their kids to do what they don't want to do. Examples are personal hygiene, getting up and ready in a timely manner, electronic use, doing chores or homework, and going to bed on time. Rather than commanding, shaming, or arguing to try and get compliance, an atmosphere of connection needs to be felt first.

It is particularly important for challenging children to not only feel connected during problem solving, but for them to feel connected while you are giving a directive. Remember that you can only influence children through connection. You can't control them through power other than using fear and intimidation which ultimately ends in a hostile confrontation.

The dialogue below is an example of a parent setting a limit with a challenging 13-year-old boy. The interaction happens the morning after the family has discussed and created a plan on how to make the morning less stressful for everyone. During the discussion, the parents acknowledged that they don't like yelling and the kids agreed that they don't like it either. The family created an Ally atmosphere by everyone working together to improve family harmony. The guidelines they agreed on state that the kids need to get ready for school before playing and no electronics in the morning.

Keep in mind that just because your kids agree to be more cooperative during the problem-solving session, this does not mean that they will follow through. When their needs are different from yours, they may forget their promise. Their prefrontal cortex is still underdeveloped, so don't get angry with them and say something like, "But you said you were going to... Why are you arguing now?" These shaming statements only hurt and make your child defensive and disconnected from you.

I warned the parents that even though they have a plan, their kids will probably not follow through with it so be prepared to use Director strategies. This is what happened, but since they were prepared, the mom was successful. First, she sets the limit and gets resistance even though she is using the highly effective It's Time Strategy. After two tries without compliance, she realizes she needs to connect, so she acknowledges her son's feelings. Then she states the expectation again and amazingly her son complies.

Her experience blew me away when I heard it because these parents came to me due to an extremely adversarial household full of arguing. You will see that by the parents learning how to connect and use language that isn't confrontational and doesn't lead to power struggles, they can immediately change their family dynamics.

Situation: My son was playing with the dog in the morning rather than getting ready for school first, which was the new family rule.

Mom: "It's time to brush your teeth and wash your face."

Child: "I will."

Mom: "It's time for personal hygiene."

Child: "I'm playing with Cody."

Mom: "It looks like Cody is having fun playing with you. You can finish playing with Cody after personal hygiene."

Mom: "My son got up and got ready without any arguing!"

The mom beautifully connects emotionally during the directive by telling her son how valuable he is to his dog. Wow. Can you imagine how good he feels about himself and his mom at this moment? Then she uses a variation of the After-Then Strategy as she states that he can continue to have fun after he completes the expectation.

Here is another example of how this mom stated the expectation, then connected with her son's feelings, and then restated the expectation. This time instead of pointing out how her son was loved by his dog she acknowledges his dislike for the rule. Both are great examples of how creative you can be when you keep in mind that emotionally connecting with your child will enable them to feel good about you because you validate their feelings. The result is more cooperation and less resistance.

> **Situation:** My son wanted to play on his phone before school.
>
> **Mom:** "The phone is off limits in the morning."
>
> **Child:** "I know."
>
> **Mom:** "I know you don't like this rule."
>
> **Child:** "I don't." (then he handed me the phone)
>
> **Mom:** "You can have it back when we get to school. Thank you for your help, our mornings are much smoother."
>
> **Child:** "I know." (and then smiled!)

If your directives are not working, check that you haven't shifted from directing as an ally to commanding as an adversary. For example, saying, "If you don't brush your teeth, then..." is a threat rather than "After you brush your teeth," which respectfully states the cause and effect of the child's actions. Also, check how connected you are to your child's experience at the moment rather than focusing on getting your needs met first. So, next time you are giving a directive and you feel the invisible wall, stop and try an empathetic response so you build influence and cooperation.

23.
Director Parenting Role: The After-Then Strategy

As a Director, you create structure to guide your children to fulfill their responsibilities, even when they don't want to. After problem solving together, or when telling them what to do, they may continue to ignore you or resist your reminders. This is the time to use an effective Director strategy.

The After-Then (or work-before-play) Strategy is one of my favorites because it is respectful and teaches children the important concept of cause and effect as well as the value of work before play. The After-Then Strategy is not an external reward system that you control, such as tallying up positive behavior and giving your child a prize in return. This is a very important distinction. The After-Then approach is effective with children as young as three and as old as twenty-three.

Chores, homework, practicing music, and bedtime routines are common activities that children need gentle guiding to complete. The After-Then approach reflects the way life truly works. After we work hard, we treat ourselves to a rest period or fun activity, such as dinner or a movie.

Take time to explain the After-Then approach before using it with your kids. It's a good idea to get kids' input about what they consider "play" as well. Kids may want to watch TV, read, or play a computer game with you for their "play" activity.

The After-Then, or when-then, statement assumes your child will do what you want her to do. Correct word order is crucial here. The first part of the directive states the child's re-sponsibilities to you or to the family. The second part states the positive result of following through with those responsibilities.

Your statement is as follows: "After you do Y (my needs or your responsibilities), then you will get X (your needs or desires)." This approach provides a positive, rather than rebel-lious, way to meet your child's need for power.

Be careful not to slip into the punishment–reward trap, which can easily happen if you feel out of control and start trying to regain control. Watch for changing word order and adding "if" to your sentence. The reward sentence structure would be, "I'll give you X (what you want) if you do Y (what I want)." A punishment statement would be, "If you don't do Y (my needs), then you can't have X (your needs)." Your use of "if" adds doubt that your child will comply, which subtly plants resistance in her mind. With punishment-reward state-ments, your tone of voice also changes from unemotional and respectful to pleading, yelling, or threatening.

When this happens, you are no longer guiding your child from your inner strength and effective structure. You shift to a position of weak authority and limited influence. When you notice this happening, stop. Breathe to calm your emotional center and restate, with certainty and clarity, what your child needs to do before they get what they want.

Here are some examples of effective After-Then statements:

"After you clean the bathroom, then you can go to your friend's house."

"After you brush your teeth, then we'll read together."

"After you pick up your toys, then you can play a video game for 20 minutes."

You may be tempted to flip the order and say, "We'll read together after you brush your teeth." You may think that telling your child what he'll get first will encourage him to comply. This shift actually puts your needs second in your child's mind, so it isn't as effective. The second part of the statement gets lost. Your child may get stuck on what he wants and respond with, "No, I want to read now."

I admit that this strategy isn't foolproof and you will need to repeat yourself, especially at first. Each time, maintain the same After-Then format and shorten it, rather than explain your reasoning.

For example:

1st directive: "After you brush your teeth, then we can play together."

Child complains.

2nd directive: "After teeth, then playtime."

Child still complains.

3rd directive: "Teeth first."

The goal is to not engage after the third directive. One dad I worked with did have to repeat more than three times but he kept calm and his son finally said, "Alright." After a few times of lengthy repeats, his children understood that dad wasn't going to change his mind or get angry as he had in the past. Now, he only states the After-Then statement once or twice.

To improve success with challenging children, you may need to add an empathetic phrase after each directive such as, "Teeth brushing isn't fun for you." Don't add "but" and moralize by saying, "Teeth brushing isn't fun for you, but you have to brush them." Remain calm and pleasant and keep practicing.

This strategy also addresses the complaint that kids are self-centered and unappreciative. A common misconception is, If I give my child what he wants, then he will think of me and give me what I want in return. This doesn't happen because children naturally think of their needs first. When parents believe reciprocity will naturally occur through their examples of kindness, children can remain self-centered and privileged while adults become hurt and angry. You're teaching the reciprocal meeting of needs with the After-Then approach. Children learn how to care for others through parents structuring many work-before-play sessions, rather than through lecturing and shaming.

The After-Then Strategy, based on the work-before-play philosophy, will become a natural part of your family, resulting in more cooperative children most of the time. Read more about how to add a connecting statement in Chapter 22, **Add Connecting to Improve Directing**, in Section 4.

24.
Stop Negotiating and State the Limit Clearly

"Why do you have to argue about everything I ask you to do? Why can't you just cooperate nicely for once? You make everything so difficult."

If your child has turned into a member of the debate team, then you are experiencing their prefrontal cortex, the logical brain, at work. Your "argumentative" child is exercising and practicing their reasoning and judgment skills. So, the next time your child doesn't comply easily, try to think to yourself, *Her brain is developing right now. How marvelous!*

The prefrontal cortex is in charge of planning, attention, judgment, reasoning, impulse control, and short-term memory. The safest place for kids to practice and develop logic is within the family. Currently, brain science asserts that the majority of neural pathway development in the prefrontal cortex is completed by age 25 for girls and age 29 for boys. So, your maturing child needs many opportunities to practice reasoning, problem solving, and debating with you.

I realize that living with a miniature attorney can be quite frustrating. To address this challenge, it is important to state clearly which issues are open for discussion and which are not. If you suddenly change from a "no-discussion" stance to an "OK, we'll talk about it" stance, your negotiating child becomes confused. This confusion then leads your child to think that every issue is open for debate.

There are three key steps required to teach kids to negotiate when appropriate and to comply without negotiation when appropriate. The first step is to determine who has ownership for making the final decision about how to resolve an issue. The final decision can be made by parent, parent and child together, or child only. Discussion and negotiation can occur when the child has full or partial ownership of the decision but not when the parent has full ownership of it. Ownership of the decision will determine whether your Parental role is as a Director (no negotiation), Collaborator (negotiation), or Supporter/Confidant (mostly listening). Read Chapter 8, *Choose Your Parental Role: Director, Collaborator, or Supporter*, in Section 1 for details.

The second step is to clarify for your children which issues are non-negotiable and which are negotiable. Issues that are non-negotiable when children are young, such as bedtime, will become negotiable as they mature. You can let your kids know that you are setting the rule for now, but when they reach a certain age, you will discuss the rule with them.

The third step for enforcing a non-negotiable guideline is to respond to your children in a manner that does not fuel negotiation. If your child continues to argue, it's because you keep the argument going. You probably respond to the "Why do I have to" questions because you think that you always need to explain your reasoning. You do not.

If your child's goal is to gain power to get what they want, then your explanation will probably not stop your child from arguing. Your child will not say, "Thank you for explaining that to me. Now I understand, and I will do what you want me to do." Don't we wish!

Recently, a mom shared with me how her daughter argues about everything and it drives her nuts. The daughter argues about taking a shower, brushing her teeth, and doing her homework. After discussing the issue further, we discovered that the mom had fallen into the negative loop of "parental explanation," which keeps the arguing going.

Instead of responding to her daughter's "why" questions, I taught her how to keep restating the directive instead. It's important to remember that this approach should be used when your child is not part of the decision-making process.

Here is how the mom responded to stop the arguing:

Mom: "It's time for a shower."

Daughter: "Why do I have to take a shower now?"

Mom: "Shower time."

Daughter: "But I don't want to take a shower."

Mom: "After you take a shower, then you can read."

Daughter: "I took one last night."

Mom: "Shower."

Daughter: "Oh, alright."

Here's an example of giving clear and respectful directives with a brief explanation and acknowledgment so you maintain connection and reduce arguing.

Parent: "It's time to walk the dog."

Daughter: "Why do I have to walk the dog?"

Parent: "He needs it. Here's his leash."

Daughter: "But I don't want to walk him. It's too cold out."

Parent: "After you walk the dog, then you can get warm and watch a show."

Daughter: "I walked him yesterday."

Parent: "Yes you did. It's time to walk him again."

Daughter: "Okay."

The key component of your response is to keep repeating the directive in various short forms. Don't give reasons to try to convince your child to agree with you. If you do, then you're debating, and this is where the problem lies. You are not in a courtroom trying to win a case. When enforcing a non-negotiable guideline, you are the Director, and you are respectfully and calmly reminding your child of what is expected. Plan to repeat yourself calmly a few times.

When directives are given in this way, children will soon understand that you are not negotiating and they will follow your lead. Make sure, though, that they also have plenty of appropriate opportunities to discuss problems and practice negotiating with you.

25.
Your Personal Boundaries Create Appreciative Children

I do so much for my children, and they just don't appreciate it. They think only about themselves. Sometimes, I feel like I'm here simply to give them what they want. Why don't they think about me?

If you're thinking this way, there's a good chance you have not set clear personal boundaries.

Personal boundaries differ from rules, or limits. Boundaries refer to what you will or will not do, whereas rules, or limits, address what you want your children to do or not do. With boundaries, you're controlling your own behavior in response to what your child does rather than directly trying to control your child's behavior.

Here are some examples of boundaries:

"I'm not able to drive you to the store now."

"I will make dinner after the kitchen is cleaned."

"I'll give you an answer after you ask nicely."

"It's too late for me to play a game with you."

"I won't pay $70 for shoes. I'll give you $35 toward the shoes."

Each boundary statement focuses on your needs and actions. Rather than trying to exercise power over your child, you are taking control over yourself. In both approaches, controlling yourself or controlling your child, the end goal is for the child to change. However, the boundary-setting approach can feel more respectful to both you and your child and avoids power struggles, as long as you stay the course. If you start out with a boundary statement, but then give in to negative reactions from your kids, you'll end up in an argument. At the start, boundary-setting requires courage and builds your confidence over time as you see positive results.

Here are the same examples from above, stated in a command format, where the parent is trying to control the child's behavior:

"I wish you had told me earlier that you need a ride. Now dinner will be late."

"Clean up the kitchen now."

"Don't talk to me in that rude tone."

"If you had gotten ready earlier, then we would've had time to play a game."

"How can you expect me to pay $70 for shoes?"

Non-boundary punitive responses usually blame and hurt the child, leading to a revenge cycle of the child hurting you back. This cycle is followed by an out-of-control power struggle. Choosing personal boundary-setting statements ensures that your needs are respected and you feel appreciated.

It can be hard to set a boundary that denies or delays your child's wants and needs. As you begin to implement boundary-setting, there will be some pushback from your children because they are accustomed to you putting your needs second. Learning how to balance whose needs are being met can be tricky. As soon as you start to feel unappreciated or disrespected, it's time to put yourself first more often through effective boundary-setting.

Putting others' needs first and being altruistic comes more naturally for some of us than for others. If your child tends to use their strength to fight for their own needs, it's imperative that you set clear boundaries in a calm and loving manner.

Be careful not to judge your child or label them as "self-centered." Rather, see your child as proud and guide them toward restraining some of their own needs and putting other's needs first, when appropriate. Instead of saying, "Don't be so selfish," which is hurtful, stick to your boundary because this is how your child will learn to be aware of others' needs, wait, and put aside their own needs for the moment.

Some children want to be overprotected and they especially need your strong and loving boundaries as well. When you say, "I'm not going to put on your clothes for you. I know you can do it," you are stating your boundary and also your confidence in your child's ability to succeed without your help. If whining follows, repeat your boundary and add what will come after getting dressed. Don't engage in an argument.

Often, it can be helpful to leave the situation with words like, "I'll see you at the breakfast table."

Here are some parental self-talk statements to remind you of the importance of boundary-setting:

- *It's essential for my child to learn how to contribute to the welfare of the family. My boundaries help teach this value.*

- *I can handle an upset child who doesn't get his way. The upsets will diminish when I am firm about my personal boundaries.*

- *I won't allow myself to feel manipulated. I will clearly state what I will or will not do and not change my mind.*

26.
How to Set Your Family's Electronics-Use Guidelines

The first step in creating your family's electronics-use guidelines is to start a family discussion about your family's current electronics use. This discussion should include children talking about parents' use of electronics as well as parents talking about children's use. The purpose of the discussion and resulting guidelines is to create greater family harmony, cooperation, and unity. Your children need to learn that each person's actions impact the other family members. No one exists in a vacuum.

Before beginning this sensitive family discussion, it's important to learn about potential communication blocks and how to listen openly. You may need more than one discussion to address questions and develop solutions.

Ultimately, you have the final say about the guidelines because you are the adult requesting limits on usage. Remember that just because kids are part of the discussion doesn't mean they will automatically follow the rules. In fact, it's better to expect that they won't. For more information on this, read the chapters about the Collaborator Role in Section 5 and the

Director Role in Section 4 to learn how to discuss ideas and ensure that guidelines are followed.

I realize that setting guidelines with teens is especially difficult. Teens let you know they don't want to be "nagged" about too much electronics use. If you're concerned that your teen may be addicted to video gaming because they've stopped doing other activities, they don't see friends as often, their grades have dropped, and/or they get angry easily, it is especially important that you set clear limits.

Below are suggested discussion questions and situations in which you would set guidelines. Try to apply the guidelines to all family members.

Ask questions such as:

1. What problems does electronics use create, whether it's for video games, Facebook, email, etc.?

2. Do you think (name of family member) uses electronics too much? Why do you say that? (For example: "I feel ignored. They don't answer me. They aren't doing what they used to do, etc.")

3. If computers are used for work in the home, are they taking the parent away from the family too much?

4. What other activities can you do instead of video gaming? Why is that important?

5. Why is it so hard to stop video gaming when asked to?

Each family is unique. Base your guidelines on your family's values about how you believe people should be treated. Put people before electronics. Clearly state and post the values behind each rule so everyone understands why you will enforce them. Your purpose is to teach your kids life skills that develop healthy relationship habits.

Set guidelines for electronics use in the following situations. In order to stimulate discussion, I have suggested a variety of usage ideas to consider for your family.

At home: Video games are played only at specified times. Video game players acknowledge people speaking to them by looking at them. Phones are turned off or silenced at specified times. Phones are ignored when they ring or receive a text, unless it's an emergency.

In the car: Phones are used only for driving directions. All other phones are placed in the trunk. No texting or reading texts while driving. Video games are played only when the car ride lasts longer than one hour.

While eating together: No electronics are brought to the table. Phones are not answered during dinner.

In the morning

School days: No video games or TV until everyone is ready. No electronics at all.

Non-school days: Physical activity or playtime before electronics are used. Set number of hours each day.

In the evening

School days: All electronics are turned in or locked up at the stated time. Only a computer with no video game access is used. Cell phones or video games are used only after chores and/or homework are completed satisfactorily.

Non-school days: After chores are done, you may use electronics for a set amount of time.

While visiting family members: You must spend a set amount of time interacting with the family before playing video games or talking on the phone. Phones are left in the car.

While at a friend's house or when a friend is visiting: After engaging in creative play for a set amount of time, then you can play video games. The friend's cell phone or game is put away in your care until that time. If the parent is not present to enforce the rules, talk beforehand about how the child likes his friends to behave when they are at his house. When you aren't at home, don't expect teens to follow the guidelines if they don't value the rules.

As a parent, you are an important role model for how to appropriately use electronics. Check your own usage before setting limits on your kids' usage. Electronics can be easily overused by everyone, resulting in less connection and more conflict between family members.

Don't ignore your gut feelings of concern or fear about your kids' cell phone usage or video gaming. You have an obligation to care for your children's well-being, and setting limits on electronics is an important part of that loving care. Your confidence in your non-negotiable rules, backed by your values and effective delivery, will create happier children and a more harmonious home.

27.
You Can Keep Video Games from Overtaking Your Family

Parents struggle with setting limits on video game playing to the point of feeling powerless. It can feel like the video game companies are controlling your children. However, you have more power than you think to keep video gaming obsession out of your home.

Whereas drug and alcohol use often begins during the teen years outside the home, video gaming can begin at a very young age right in front of your eyes. Since alcohol and drugs are illegal for kids, it is easier for us to set clear limits around them. In contrast, video games are pushed on children and adults as being beneficial, fun, and a way to be socially savvy.

Let's explore why it's hard to set limits on video games and how you can make sure your kids aren't chained to the computer or smartphone. This chain doesn't appear overnight. It is created link by link. You can make conscious efforts to not build the links and take strong action now to break the existing chain.

Video games are a great way to keep kids occupied. In contrast to limiting movies or TV, however, limiting games can evoke extreme anger and disrespect from children. We must take this problem seriously because video games are made to stimulate the release of the feel-good chemical dopamine in the pleasure center of the brain, which can lead to obsessive gaming. Anyone can experience pleasure while playing video games due to the intensity of competition in games and the rewards of winning. Everyday life cannot compete with the excitement of gaming, thus the growing obsession with the unreal world can lead to rejecting the real world.

A link in the addictive chain is created when you habitually give your kids a tablet or smartphone at the grocery store, in the car, or any time you want quiet. The decision to hand over a smartphone or tablet is an understandable one because our lives are pleasant when kids are totally engaged in a video game. This momentary ease, however, can lead to long-term problems down the line such as:

Parent problems:
- Not communicating with children, which leads to significant barriers with teens

- Not learning how to teach children self-regulation and self-control

- Losing parental authority

Child problems:
- Expecting to play games and no longer asking - they reach for the computer or smartphone first thing in the morning

- Getting bored easily without the intense brain stimulation from games

- Being less creative or less able to think about life

- Resisting physical play outdoors and not learning the emotional benefits of connecting with nature and with others

Many parents express deep concern about the addictive nature of video games and report beginning to see signs of addiction as early as age 10. Parents and experts report the following signs of addiction in children:

- Getting angry and belligerent with parents when limits are enforced

- Losing track of time and interest in previously important activities or hobbies

- Becoming socially isolated, moody, or irritable

- Neglecting schoolwork and struggling to achieve acceptable grades

- Complaining that they have nothing to do when they aren't playing a video game

Due to their addictive nature and potential for many long-term problems, it is essential to determine your rules and limits regarding video games and post them, along with your reasoning, in your home. Tell your kids, "We realize that we need to set clearer guidelines about electronics use. The rules will be different than what you are used to. We know they will make our family happier." Here are some suggestions to consider:

- No video games in the car except for trips over… (1 hour, 2 hours).

- No video games in the morning until everyone is ready for the day.

- No video games at the dinner table - eat dinner together at least 4 nights during the week.

- No video games on a school night - restrict phone and TV usage.

- On the weekends, kids must do creative play before doing video games.

- Computer or phone gaming must be done with the bedroom door open or in a common room.

When enforcing rules, it is essential to stay strong and stick to your limits. Once you have shared your rules and your reasons for them, you do not need to repeat them when your child asks you, "Why?" Just point to your posted sign. Never give in or negotiate with your children. Tell them that the rules are non-negotiable.

Children are good at getting what they want by trying to make you doubt your decisions. They may say that you don't care about them, tell you that all their friends are playing the game, or threaten that they won't do what you want unless you let them play more. Never doubt yourself. Instead, tell yourself, *I love my children, and I know what's best for them. The prefrontal cortexes in their brains are immature and need-driven. I am keeping the limit for my children's safety and my family's happiness. I will not argue or give in. I will feel good about myself.*

One of my clients, the mother of a teenage son, took the computer away from her son so he couldn't sit in his room and play interactive games with his headphones on. He still had his smartphone, yet he couldn't play intense interactive games. He became more pleasant and cooperative. To his mom's amazement, he didn't even ask for the computer back. During school, he now uses a computer that is blocked from any video gaming.

Another mom set a one-hour video game limit on the weekend with her 9 year-old son. She gave him a five-minute warning and then said, "It's time to end." He started complaining and saying, "One more minute." She became angry because she felt disrespected. She had explained the new rule, he had agreed, and now he was arguing. I encouraged her to expect resistance and to be prepared to continue staying strong with the limit. One option is to restate the limit, "It's time to stop. Give me the device." You may need to reduce your words. Simply putting out your hand and saying, "Phone," can be effective.

Another limit setting approach is to base your child's privilege of playing on their response to being told to stop. This is setting your personal boundary of how you expect to be treated. You want your child to understand that if they stop playing without any arguing, then they get to play the next scheduled time. If they argue with you and ask for more time, then they lose the privilege of playing the next scheduled time. They can try again the time after that. It's crucial that your child clearly understands this expectation ahead of time.

Do not give in or give your child another chance, no matter how much they plead, until the next gaming time.

Don't extend the current time and make sure to set a reminder so you don't forget this change. It could sound like this:

Parent: "It's time to end playing."

Child: "Just one more minute."

Parent: "Remember the rule. Since you are arguing now, you won't be allowed to play on... (Whenever the next scheduled time is.) You can try stopping without arguing the time after that."

Then, put out your hand to receive the electronic device or to close the computer. Expect grumbling as your child hands you the device and then walk away. Do not engage in a physical or verbal tug-of-war. When you calmly set the limit without shaming and hurting your child, they will see you as the authority and they won't try to get revenge by hurting you in return. Shaming words are, "I shouldn't have to tell you again," "It's your fault," or "Don't blame me for losing your privilege."

Push down the fear that this strategy isn't going to work because you haven't been successful in the past. Remember, the key to changing your child's behavior is to change your side of the parent-child equation first, your thoughts and actions, in order to bring out a more positive response from your child. Keep in mind that limit setting is more effective when you have spent time listening and connecting to your child during non-limit setting times. Structuring and nurturing the relationship are equally important.

Each limit you set with your child will keep the addictive chain from growing and break the current chain. Bear in mind that you are setting the example for your children, so you must follow the rules around technology as well in order to ensure compliance from them.

28.
The Importance of Chores and How to Get Them Done

Most parents know chores are important, but getting them done is another matter. It's an additional hassle when teenagers are so loaded with homework and activities to the point that parents easily use, "They're too busy," as an excuse to let the chores slide.

However, doing chores teaches children that everyone's contribution to the family is important for creating a unified household. Even if you have paid help, each child needs to have chores. Doing tasks builds their sense of being capable, belonging, and feeling connected to a family, which leads to higher self-esteem. Our basic need for family connection cannot be gained through school or doing homework.

When your children leave home, at some point, they will be living with people who will expect them to contribute to the well-being of the household. If they haven't learned the proper skills from you, they won't know how to meet these new expectations. As a result of their lack of practice, their inability to contribute responsibly will cause their housemates to be unhappy with them. These disgruntled housemates will complain so your child will feel bad about himself. So, when you want to give your kids a break from chores because they're "too busy," realize that you're taking away a necessary opportunity for them to develop self-esteem and become responsible adults.

Chore management involves a two-step learning process. First, use the Collaborator Role problem-solving process to teach how to discuss ideas and find solutions together. Second, use the Director Role processes to teach your kids how to follow through with their commitments. If your children enjoy chores, then posting a chore chart will be sufficient. However, if your children don't like chores, it is your responsibility to use effective strategies to ensure that chores are completed so your children learn the values of taking responsibility and work before play.

The Collaborator Problem-Solving Process

Start by telling your kids that chores will be distributed more evenly in the family and that they will participate in dividing up the chores fairly. Before you meet as a family, post a sheet of paper where everyone can write down chores so that when you have your problem-solving meeting, you already have a list of chores with which to start. This will make the meeting shorter. Set a timer for 30 minutes so the kids know that the meeting won't go on forever. During this meeting, your goal is to complete the list of chores, listen to everyone's thoughts and feelings about chores, and divide up the chores.

When your children see the long list of chores you do that they take for granted, such as driving them places, going grocery shopping, preparing the meals, and buying clothes, they will see the inequity and be more willing to help. Decide together how to design and display the completed chore chart, whether chores will rotate, and whether trading and sharing chores will be allowed.

You may want to complete a signed agreement about the chores. Also, pick a date one week later to meet again and determine whether the plan worked, or if another plan should be tried. When you've accomplished the first step of the problem-solving process together, congratulate your family for discussing ideas, listening to each other, and deciding on a solution to try. Chore completion is a separate process to celebrate.

The Director Strategies Follow-Through Process

Ensuring follow-through is the second step of the chore management learning process. This step is primarily your responsibility to manage. Even if creating the chore chart is fun for younger kids, ensuring follow-through is the bigger challenge for adults. Don't assume that because your kids have made a plan with you and signed an agreement, they automatically know how to follow through with doing something they don't want to do. Learning about work before play is a crucial life skill. To teach this skill, use Director strategies to guarantee follow-through.

Read my suggested strategies earlier in this section to learn how to give directions that are followed without negotiating, threatening, or engaging in a power struggle. As a parent, my favorite strategy was the After-Then approach. I would keep in mind what my teenage daughter had to do (the work) so that when she requested to play, I would use the After-Then Strategy. Because I used this strategy consistently, I didn't have to repeat myself too many times. For more information, read Chapter 23, *Director Parenting Role: After-Then Strategy.*

Here is an example of how I would implement the After-Then Strategy with my daughter:

Jen: "Mom, can I go to Diana's house?"

Me: "After you clean the bathroom, then you can go."

Jen: "But Mom, she wants me to go there now and doing the bathroom will take too long."

Me: "After the bathroom, you can go."

Jen: "Mommmmm!"

Me: "Bathroom first."

Jen: "Why didn't you tell me sooner?"

Me: No response.

Jen: "Oh, alright."

Bingo! No arguing, no yelling, and no hurt feelings. My daughter wanted to get her needs met, and I insisted that she do the work before the play.

Parents get upset when their kids have signed a chores agreement but won't do the chores because parents don't understand that discussing ideas and developing internal motivation are two different processes. Be careful not to use shaming to try to get your kids to cooperate. Examples of hurtful shaming and humiliating statements are, "You said you were going to do them," "You're being irresponsible," "I can't rely on you," "Why do I have to remind (nag) you so much?" "You need to help around here," "I do so much," and on and on. Using respectful Director Parenting Role strategies without unrealistic expectations that kids should do chores without direction will create a more harmonious home with more cooperative and thoughtful children.

As children mature and practice doing chores, they learn to push themselves to do undesirable tasks on their own. This inner motivation may not develop in some areas until they're adults, yet rest assured that your insistence on chores has laid an important foundation for taking responsibility and cooperating with others for life.

29.
Dad Sets Clear Expectations and Learns to Use Empathy

Setting clear expectations with a strong-willed child can be challenging. When they're young, they have big tantrums that parents often want to avoid. This desire to avoid tantrums creates a pattern of parents giving in to appease the tantrum rather than remaining firm and implementing the clear, strong limit the child needs.

The following real-life coaching scenario involves a dad, Ben, learning how to set limits and boundaries with his strong-willed nine-year-old daughter, Julia. In the email exchange below, Ben shared his success and then asked me for additional advice. While he did an excellent job setting his personal boundaries and limits for his daughter, Ben did not establish the emotional connection that would lead to future improved cooperation.

Oftentimes, parents become concerned that if they are compassionate with their kids, they won't be able to hold the boundary or limit. To address this concern, I recommend practicing firmness and compassion together, which leads to incredibly positive results.

Below is Ben's email with my return email containing my coaching comments in bold. I have also indicated what parenting strategy he was using.

All names have been changed for confidentiality purposes.

Hi, Cynthia.

I would like to relay an example of an interaction I had with Julia this past weekend. I welcome your input!

On Saturday, my wife left early in the morning to go to a training session for Girl Scouts. I asked a babysitter (Mary) to come to our house to help with the kids since there were a couple of activities going on that morning.

The plan was to pick up Tommy from a birthday party at 11:30 in San Mateo and then drive to Goodwill to drop off a carload of donated items. After that, we were planning to go to the county fair, which Julia was looking forward to.

The Goodwill donation was from the Girl Scouts. My wife had left instructions that Julia needed to make a sign saying, "Gift from Girl Scouts Troop ******," and wear her sash while holding the sign in front of Goodwill.

Julia refused to make the sign. I simply said, "Sign and sash and then we leave." **(Limit implied in an After-Then Strategy)** I needed to make a phone call, so I went downstairs for about 20 minutes. When I came back up, she had made the sign but had not gotten her sash.

Julia refused to look for the sash. She got in the car and said, "I won't wear the sash. It doesn't matter. Let's just go." I reiterated, "When you bring your sash, then we can leave," *(The After-Then Strategy)* but she refused to get out of the car to get the sash. We were running late, and we needed to pick up Tommy at 11:30 exactly. Fortunately, the sitter (Mary) was there. So, in light of Julia's refusal, I asked Mary to pick up Tommy. It took a lot of focus to stay calm and not threaten Julia.

Congratulations on your self-control, Ben!

At this point, since Tommy was being picked up, here is where you could have taken the opportunity to connect emotionally with Julia by using empathy. For example, "I can see that you definitely don't want to wear your sash. I'm wondering why you're so resistant." Then PAUSE and give her space to share her reasons and feelings.

You're not asking her, "Why don't you want to wear the sash?" Instead, you're wondering. A direct question can feel like an interrogation communication block, which is why I avoid them. If you had used the Wondering Strategy, Julia probably would have shared her feelings about the sash sooner because she would have felt you were her ally. This approach would have changed the remainder of the interaction.

Let's now review what you did say to your daughter.

I said, "I'm going inside. I hope you will come get your sash." *(Boundary then expectation)*

I went inside and was able to find her sash. Julia had come back inside from the car as well. I said, "Oh, here is your sash." She was calm and said, "OK, fine. I'll put it on here but not outside the house. I don't have any badges on my sash, and everyone else does. Also, the troop number is wrong on my sash." *(Great that you could engage in problem solving together at this point. You didn't belittle Julia by telling her not to worry about it.)*

We devised a plan for Julia to use the sign she had made to cover up the incorrect troop number on her sash.

We got in the car, met up with Mary and Tommy, and then proceeded to Goodwill. When we arrived, Julia initially refused to put on her sash. I calmly *(Fantastic!)* explained that the sash was part of her commitment to her troop. *(Limit)* She put it on, I took a photo, and we left in pretty good shape.

Here is Ben's self-evaluation along with my comments.

I think a couple of things worked pretty well:

Simply telling Julia what needed to happen (make the sign, wear the sash)

I was really tempted to use threats to try to make her comply, but was able to stay calm and avoid anything beyond the statement of what needed to happen. **(Much better to use influence rather than forcing power and control)**

I gave her the space to make her own decision. I didn't say, "This must happen now," which I think might have prompted her to dig in her heels. **(I agree.)**

You can set an expectation or limit while also empathizing and then reset the limit or engage in problem solving as you did. This actually works better than just being "stern."

Great implementation of the skills you're learning!

I suggest that you study communication blocks, listening openly, and empathetic statements to build more competence with these skills.

Congratulations, Ben.

Cynthia

30.
Parent Success Stories in the Director Role

Work With Your Child to Build Cooperation and Better Behavior

My son is 9 years old and loves to argue with me. He wants to challenge and disagree with everything I say. For example, if I tell him not to lean on the rope in the water, he'll lean on it just to let me know who's boss. I came to Cynthia for help because using time-outs and taking things away weren't working and made our relationship worse. Cynthia suggested that I work with Jack's nature. She said that kids like my son do better with facts and encouragement rather than attempts to control.

The day after meeting with Cynthia, I wanted my son to sit farther away from the TV. Rather than saying, "Move back," I decided to give him information about the possible damage to his eyes that sitting too close to the TV could cause. He responded by moving back and asking me if he was far enough away! I couldn't believe it. There was no fighting, and I got the result I wanted. Learning how to work with my child rather than working against and controlling him definitely gets the results I want and makes my son and me feel good about one another. Thanks, Cynthia!

Creating More Cooperation With My Daughter

I'm a mom of three children, ages 7, 5, and 3.

I contacted Cynthia primarily because of my 5-year-old daughter's screaming and my screaming in return. I wanted to learn how to discipline my children more effectively so that they would cooperate. I also wanted a much better relationship with my daughter. I've been working with Cynthia for over three months now with amazing results.

Cynthia understands the source of my negative behavior as well as my daughter's, so she can teach me the best solutions possible.

Through her parenting education process, I am making permanent positive changes in my interactions with my children.

Here is an example of how I changed my response to my daughter's yelling and refusal to cooperate:

Recently, I was trying to make my daughter get ready for bed because it was late. I was focusing on my fears about what would happen if she didn't go to bed. She resisted my "coaxing" and made controlling statements like, "I'll come when I want to."

In the past, I would have stayed stuck in my own thoughts, yelled louder, and started threatening her with consequences.

If I yelled, she would have continued to yell back at me. She might have finally come to bed, yet the result would have been an awful feeling between us. I would've been considered the "mean mommy."

Through Cynthia's wisdom and knowledge and my continual practice, this time I was able to stop myself from yelling.

Instead, I said, "I'm going to take care of your brother. Come to bed when you're ready." I walked away calmly, and she soon followed. She felt powerful, and I didn't engage in the power struggle. I could understand myself, which led to managing my own emotional triggers.

This is just one example of how I've gone from believing I'll never be able to change to actually making changes that feel good and building closer relationships with my kids. I'm looking forward to continuing to work with Cynthia to create a harmonious home.

Parents Turn a Chaotic Home Into a Cooperative Home

When my husband and I first sought Cynthia's help, our home was a pretty chaotic place. We have three kids, and we were having difficulty getting them to do their chores and take accountability for their actions without threats of taking away screen time, cell phones, or play time. These threats and punishments didn't seem to change their behaviors over time, and my frustration as a parent was building.

I had attended two of Cynthia's seminars over the past few years, and what she said made a lot of sense to me, but I wasn't sure how to implement her strategies over a sustained period of time. My husband and I decided to invest the time and money in her individual parenting coaching program. Working one-on-one with Cynthia has made a huge difference in how we parent and how our kids respond to us. We learned how to set better personal boundaries, which of our behaviors cause our kids to tune us out, and how to engage with our kids in a more productive way.

It's been a real blessing, especially for my relationship with my teenage daughter. Our daughter was having a hard time, and we couldn't figure out how to guide and support her. We were getting caught up in her behavior and weren't able to see what was behind it or how to deal with it. Through our sessions with Cynthia, we were able to create an effective plan and structure that helped our daughter become more independent, develop life skills, and improve her mood and outlook on the world. She and I have a better relationship because of our time with Cynthia, and I feel more confident to go through the teenage years with our kids because of the tools I've learned from Cynthia. I know that we will continue to check in with Cynthia over the years to stay on track and continue growing as parents.

Thanks, Cynthia!

Setting Clear Expectations and Listening Were Key to My Success

I'm a mother of five girls, ages 7 to 22. I was having difficulty with my 13-year-old daughter who wasn't talking with me, wasn't cooperative, and was disrespectful. I worked with Cynthia for three months and learned so much more than I expected. Cynthia was easy to work with, and everything I learned from her was useful and valuable.

I felt that Cynthia could really understand where I was coming from. I appreciated hearing about her experiences with her own daughter. She always gave me examples of how to say things to my kids, like a script to guide me. Cynthia encouraged me in a way that made me feel like I could make changes. Here is a story of an impactful interaction with my daughter that Cynthia helped me learn from and change. I will never forget this.

After I started working with Cynthia, I went home one afternoon with the expectation that my daughter would've cleaned up the kitchen. When I got home, though, there was a mess. I lost it and started yelling at my daughter. "You don't want to help. Don't you see this mess? I can't handle this alone. You don't care about what needs to be done. You're driving me crazy." She started to cry and clean, and I continued with, "This could've been done in ten minutes."

Yelling at my daughter was really bad, and I felt horrible afterwards. My husband told me that my response set us back in the progress we had been making. I shouldn't have blown up at her.

Cynthia and I reviewed what I was thinking that lead to my anger. I was labeling my daughter as selfish and inconsiderate and thinking that she only cared about what she wanted to do, not what I wanted her to do. Because of these thoughts, I felt irritated, hurt, upset, disappointed, and abandoned, which led to my hurtful words.

Cynthia and I discussed what my daughter might be thinking and feeling during my outburst. Perhaps she thought, *My mom thinks I'm selfish. She's disappointed in me. It's unfair that I'm being yelled at and my sisters aren't, because they didn't clean either. She didn't ask me to clean the kitchen.*

My scolding probably caused my daughter to feel overwhelmed, ashamed, discouraged, embarrassed, frustrated, rejected, and unloved. She stood there crying, and I felt so embarrassed and ashamed about my outburst.

I had to change and make amends with her. Cynthia and I discussed some more flexible and compassionate thoughts I could have about my daughter. Some ideas were: *At age 13, it's normal for her not to think on her own about what needs to be done. I didn't ask her to clean. I know she cares. I just expected that she would clean without being told, which wasn't right. I need to find a better way to teach her how to contribute to the family. In the future, I will clarify my expectations in a loving and nonjudgmental way. When I approach my daughter this way, I can trust her to do what I ask of her.*

I started making amends by apologizing, and the best way to do that was to write my daughter a letter. She was so upset with me that she didn't want to listen to me. By writing the letter, she could re-read it when she felt less upset. In the letter, I acknowledged that I assumed my daughter knew my expectations as though she could read my mind. That wasn't fair, and in the future, I promised to be clear. I apologized for yelling and blaming her 100% for the kitchen not being cleaned. I acknowledged other communication failures as well, such as saying and thinking, "You should know better," which is judgmental and hurtful.

From this experience, I learned how to change my beliefs and words. Now, I have compassion for my daughter, and I clearly state my expectations. Recently, my daughter had a few friends over, and they were baking in the kitchen. I went out, and before I left, I told her to clean the kitchen when she and her friends were done. Before I came home, I texted her, "Make sure to do a complete cleanup of the kitchen before I get home." When I got home, the kitchen was spotless, even though my daughter had her friends with her. I was amazed. Now, my daughter is more responsible about doing the dishes on her designated nights without being told. If she does need a reminder because she left the table and went to her room while the rest of the family was still eating, we give her a gentle one such as, "Honey, we're done now so you can do the dishes." She gets up and does them, even though she's in the middle of an activity, with acceptable grumbling.

Another key skill I learned was to stop using the communication blocks of interrogating and psychologizing. Since I've stopped using these blocks, my daughter is more open and is sharing more with us. Because I now know how to listen, my daughter is kinder to me, her dad, and her younger sister. These previous problem areas have all improved.

Thank you, Cynthia, for showing me the path to changing myself and creating a happier and more harmonious home.

Section 5

The Collaborator and Supporter Roles – Solving Problems

31.
Teach Children How to Successfully Handle Life's Challenges

Parents love their children and want them to be happy, protected, and successful. Problems occur, though, when parents control their children too much instead of teaching them independent thinking skills that develop responsibility. Because of parents' fear, they rush in to solve their children's problems and take away their pain rather than watch them struggle.

Rescuing, overprotecting, doing too much, and even lying for your child weakens her self-esteem because these actions send the message that she is not capable of managing her life. While it's true that her ability may be limited now, it will increase with age. Even five-year-olds can think about problems and find solutions with your guidance, not your control. Every time you take away a problem-solving opportunity, your child's self-esteem diminishes. You will know she feels incapable and defeated when she says, "You think I'm stupid," "You think I can't figure it out," or "You think I'm dumb."

Even though it's heart-wrenching to hear these statements, don't jump in and say, "Of course I don't think that." Rather, understand that your actions have sent this unintentional message, and now it's time to change. Instead, say, "I realize I've been acting as if you don't have your own ideas. I'm learning how to solve our problems together and support you as you make your own decisions." With this new framework, you can learn how to be the Collaborator when you and your child are struggling together or the Supporter when your child is struggling alone. Thus, rather than feeling badly about himself, your child will think, *My parent believes I have good ideas and will listen to me. I'm so glad I have a parent to help me.*

There are four common ways that parents weaken children which cause them to become immobilized and afraid to challenge themselves and confront problems:

1. Doing too much for them: As children mature, it's crucial to ensure that they take on more responsibility for their daily lives. Don't let their complaints stop you from having them make their own lunches, get themselves up on time, do their own laundry, and make important decisions, as well as other activities that develop confidence and self-esteem.

2. Giving them too much: Be wary of giving your children too much to make up for your own childhood or compete with other parents. I hear many complaints about kids expecting too much and not appreciating what parents do for them. These complaints are a red flag that you're giving too much without expectations in return and not setting your personal boundaries.

3. Overprotecting/rescuing: Children need adults who can handle hearing their upsets without rescuing

them or shaming them for their mistakes. Your child's life won't be damaged if they forget their lunch or their homework one day. Instead of overprotecting or rescuing your child, let her experience how cause-and-effect impacts her life. Manage your own emotional triggers that cause you to weaken your child even though you believe you are helping her.

4. **Lying for them/making excuses for their behavior:** No parent easily acknowledges that his child is lying, hurting others, or is unsuccessful, which is why parents jump in and blame teachers, coaches, or other adults rather than accept their child's shortcomings. During a dispute with others, an Ally parent doesn't automatically take her child's side. Rather, as an ally, you accept all aspects of your child with courage and confidence that improvement will happen with your guidance. Automatically defending your child teaches him to not take responsibility for his actions, which is opposite of what you want. Developmentally, teenagers are masters at lying to meet their needs, so don't take their misbehavior personally. Rather, use your intuition along with your logical brain to discern the truth and solve problems as a Director, Collaborator, or Supporter.

When we strengthen our children, they develop courage and high self-esteem. As we teach them problem-solving skills, keep the following points in mind:

1. Turn control of their own lives over to your children as soon as possible. When your children say, "I can do it," give them many opportunities to practice as you

patiently support them in a non-controlling manner. Your parental role is to prepare your children for life, not to make life easy for them.

2. Hang in there when the going gets tough. Intellectually, you know that children struggle and make mistakes. When you see them making choices that cause you to cringe, it's crucial that you continue to be their ally and believe in them because they are your children.

3. Let your children face their mistakes and use them as an opportunity to grow. Be aware of your inner fears that could cause you to rescue or shame your children in an attempt to relieve your sympathetic suffering. Love them unconditionally, as you want to be loved, and keep in mind that:

Problems = Struggle
Struggle = Growth
Growth = Wisdom
Wisdom = A Successful Life

4. Share how their actions affect others. As you share, avoid shaming, blaming, and communication blocks that make your child feel bad about himself. Instead, express the impact of his actions in a factual manner to reduce the chance of your child becoming defensive. Then, allow him time alone to process what you said rather than interrogate him to get an admission of guilt or an apology in the moment.

To follow the problem-solving path of either the Collaborator Parenting Role or the Supporter Parenting Role, focus on teaching your children how to think about their lives and how to make healthy decisions. Avoid controlling your children and causing them to put up walls of defiance that prevent you from being able to influence them. To determine how much you are teaching versus controlling your children, ask yourself the following questions: *How many minutes a day do I spend listening to my children so that they can explore their beliefs and feelings and think about possible ways to solve their struggles? How many minutes a day do I tell them what to do, get annoyed or frustrated with their behavior, or, without meaning to, criticize them?* Work toward listening more than telling.

To get started, when a challenge arises, first determine who is responsible for solving the problem. Refer to Chapter 8, **Choose Your Parental Role: Director, Collaborator, or Supporter**, in Section 1. If it's a problem that both you and your child want to solve, follow the guidelines for the Collaborator Parenting Role in Chapter 32, **Finding Solutions Together: The Collaborator Role.**

If it's your child's challenge to solve, follow the guidelines for the Supporter Parenting Role in Chapter 38, **How to Be Your Child's Trusted Supporter and Confidant**, so that your child can draw upon your strength, wisdom, and guidance to find successful solutions. Both chapters are located in this section.

Because the world is so challenging now, there is an urgent need to teach our children how to think more than how to obey.

As you listen and have dialogue with your children, they develop their prefrontal cortex, or their thinking brain. Science has shown when we verbalize our thoughts to a good listener, we release emotions that are blocking productive thinking, and develop greater insight and, therefore, better solutions.

We still need to set guidelines to ensure our children's safety, yet I propose focusing just as much, if not more, on learning how to listen to and support our children during challenging times. This focus creates a relationship of mutual trust and respect that allows your children to open their hearts to your words of wisdom. They will bask in your love and build a solid foundation of self-confidence for a lifetime.

32.
Finding Solutions Together:
The Collaborator Role

When you and your children have a problem to solve together, choose the Collaborator Parenting Role and follow the Joint-Problem-Solving Process. Examples of problems to be solved together include getting out of the house on time, completing homework, and planning a vacation. The Joint-Problem-Solving Process, based on Dr. Michael Popkin's work, teaches and develops reasoning, judgment, planning, evaluation, cooperation, consensus-building, impulse control, and memory, all of which are important life skills that are developed in the prefrontal cortex of the brain.

Before you can discuss solutions, however, you will need to establish an emotional connection with your children. The first two steps of the five-step process deserve undivided attention and are one, stop blocking communication and two, listen openly to feelings. Detailed information and strategies regarding these two essential steps can be found in Section 2, Creating Open Communication.

Your child's ability to solve problems will vary depending on their age, intellectual maturity, and whether they have any special needs that make feeling and showing empathy, paying attention, or following through difficult for them. The Joint-Problem-Solving Process is a guideline for you to alter as needed. The five steps of the process are:

1. Stop blocking communication

2. Listen openly to feelings

3. Discuss and evaluate ideas

4. Make a plan together

5. Follow up to determine success and try another idea, if needed

Step 1: Stop Blocking Communication

In an attempt to "help" kids, adults often use words that shut down communication, which can lead to anger and hurt feelings. A communication block, as defined by Michael Popkin, PhD, is any remark or attitude by the listener that injures the speaker's self-esteem enough to break communication.

Examples of blocks are commanding, giving unwanted advice, placating, interrogating, distracting, psychologizing, sarcasm, moralizing, being a know-it-all, me-tooism, and yelling. For more details on how to avoid communication blocks, study Chapter 10, *Awareness of Communication Blocks is The First Step* and Chapter 12, *Why Kids Reject Our Help – and How to Win Their Trust*, in Section 2.

Step 2: Listen Openly to Feelings

The crucial step of listening develops empathy as well as a deeper level of connection and influence between you and your child. Children, and adults, cannot discuss ideas while in an emotional state. They will refuse to "move on" and make a plan with you until you have listened respectfully and responded in an empathetic and nonjudgmental way to their thoughts and feelings. For details on how to listen openly and with empathy, study these chapters in Section 2: *The Emotional Support Process Connects You to Your Child*, *Empathy Improves Connection and Communication*, and *Parent Success Stories of Using Empathetic Responses*.

Your gift of listening provides an opportunity for better self-understanding, which will lead to improved problem solving in step three of the process. Delay any evaluation of ideas until then.

Here are examples of adult responses that can build connection and release your child's emotional tension:

"I'm sorry to hear that."

"That seems really hard."

"You seem frustrated (hurt, upset, etc.)."

"Wow."

"That sounds like a real problem."

"It's hard to know what to do."

"I can see why you're upset (want to quit, are having a hard time, don't want to do it, etc.)."

"Mmm."

"I'm here if you need me."

"It looks like you've worked hard."

Step 3: Discuss and Evaluate Ideas

Rather than promote your idea, remember that you and your child will decide on a plan together. Keep the following thoughts in mind during this process:

- *One of the greatest life skills I can teach my child is how to face problems and solve them rather than be afraid and defeated by them.*

- *My role is to encourage dialogue rather than advise.*

- *We learn from our "mistakes," so if the first solution doesn't work, we'll try another solution.*

Here are some examples of problem-solving statements and questions:

"Let's think about what we could do and the possible results of each choice."

"It's hard to know the best solution right away."

"It's important that we both agree to try the solution."

"Let's take turns coming up with different solutions. What's your first idea?"

"That's one possible solution. What do you think could happen if we tried that?"

"Just take a guess."

"What's another possible idea?"

"There's no right answer, so we can come up with many possibilities."

"I don't feel comfortable with that solution, so I want to cross that one off."

"Of the ideas we've come up with, which one do you agree to try first?"

"We'll try it for a week (___ days) and then have another meeting to see if it's working for both of us."

Step 4: Make a Plan Together

As you discuss possible solutions, you will evaluate each idea and decide together which one to try first. Remember to not push your agenda, rather be open to trying your child's suggestion, if you think it could work. Being the one who offered the chosen suggestion will boost your child's self-esteem and cause them to be more willing to participate in the necessary follow-through. Many plans, such as doing chores and homework, are most successfully carried out when they are written down, signed by all parties, and then posted for everyone to see.

Sometimes, you won't need to write down your plan. One of my clients, a father, was having difficulty in the mornings with his nine-year-old daughter, which resulted in them leaving late, thereby making him late for work. The father shared openly with his daughter how her dawdling in the morning was the problem, and he asked for her help. He was amazed to see that she didn't become defensive at his request but instead felt proud that she could help get her dad to work on time. As a result, she took responsibility in the morning without any reminders and without a written plan.

Creating the plan is the first half of step four and encouraging follow-through is the second half. Make sure to read Chapter 33, *The Three Levels of Collaborative Problem Solving*, to understand your child's level of interest in solving the problem. Your child's interest level will determine how much you will need to direct them after the plan is created.

My and many parents' favorite strategy for children who have no interest in problem solving is to use the After-Then Director parenting strategy that you'll learn about in Chapter 23, *Director Parenting Role: The After-Then Strategy*, in Section 4. Be sure to read the other chapters about the Director Role for more ideas. Remember that changing behavior patterns takes time, so be patient and compassionate. Check yourself to make sure you don't take over the problem solving or expect too much.

Step 5: Follow Up to Determine Success

During the planning session in step four, schedule a time for a follow-up meeting to determine whether the solution worked. The length of the trial period will depend on how long you're willing to be patient and let the plan unfold. During this trial period, don't jump in and make changes. When you meet for the follow-up session, congratulate each other on your success or make another plan. Don't be angry if the first solution doesn't work, because you are teaching that we don't always find the best solution the first time and that it's important to try again.

Continually seek out opportunities to solve problems together rather than tell your kids what to do. Problem solving develops self-esteem, so allow many opportunities to struggle, fail, and win.

33.
The Three Levels of Collaborative Problem Solving

Finding solutions together with your children is challenging. Maybe you don't know how to start the process, your children won't respond, or even if you do develop a plan, their enthusiasm wanes quickly, and you're left feeling discouraged. Common Collaborator discussion topics are homework, chores, vacations, getting and having a job, and college planning. Basically, the Collaborator Role applies to any situation in which you and your child are both directly impacted by the decision.

Generally speaking, you use the Collaborator Role when both you and your children want to find a solution to a problem. This is joint ownership. However, the level of commitment a child feels about actually doing the plan varies according to their interest level. When you understand their interest level and work within these limitations, you will be able to find a satisfactory solution.

There are three levels of buy-in, or interest, that you can experience with your child in the problem-solving process. The first level is the easiest and applies when your child has full interest in successfully solving the challenge. For example, you may have a child who gets upset when you don't leave for school on time. So, when you create a good plan together, she will want to follow it without the need for direction. Perhaps your child wants to get his homework done but lacks a good plan and needs help devising one. In both scenarios, once a plan is created, the child will follow it with little reminding from you because he has full interest. This is what parents want and often expect.

However, if you aren't getting good follow-through from your child, then the problem belongs in either the partial-interest level or no-interest level category. A child with partial interest wants to fix the problem, yet he doesn't have enough internal motivation to follow the agreed upon plan. He will be engaged with you in the Joint-Problem-Solving Process and will feel relieved to finally have a plan. Still, when it's time to follow through, he lacks inner motivation and maturity. This is the time to use Director Parenting Role strategies to set external guidelines for him to follow until he can develop his own inner motivation as a guide.

The least successful Collaborator plans occur when your child has no interest in following the plan. Chore completion is a good example of this category. You want to teach your child the value of doing chores now as part of the family as well as for their future happiness, so you have a family meeting, and chores are assigned. Doing chores directly affects children because it teaches them the responsibility they need to become a successful adult. They don't realize this, though, so they ignore the chore chart.

As a result, parents become mad or scared and push their no-interest child even more, which results in greater resistance. This negative parent-child interaction becomes a vicious power struggle cycle that leaves everyone feeling frustrated. Areas of no-interest vary from showering, which has an immediate negative impact, to completing a college application, which could have a long-term negative impact on your child.

You can tell your child doesn't have any interest in solving a problem when they won't talk to you, tell you to leave them alone, become angry with you, or use other forms of avoidance. The goal of avoidance could be triggered by your child feeling overwhelmed, discouraged, or not valuing the problem. To get through this avoidance wall and be a successful Collaborator, it's essential to spend as much time as is necessary listening to your child with empathy before attempting to discuss solutions. Becoming a skilled empathetic listener requires inner transformation on your part to the point where you believe that your child's happiness is more important than her making you happy. She must feel that you are her ally, and as an ally, you are open to solutions outside your own comfort zone.

An extreme case of no-interest occurred when my own daughter didn't value tedious homework that didn't contribute to her knowledge. Because she didn't value it, she wouldn't discuss a homework completion plan, and we couldn't make her do it. This was difficult to accept, but once we put her happiness ahead of our expectations, we discussed alternative options with an Ally perspective. We used the Collaborator process to find a high school that matched her values. As a result of changing schools, she completed high school, attended an appropriate college, and is now financially able to support herself while living in a major metropolitan area. We let go of the fear that made us believe there was only one path to success, and instead, we found the best path for our daughter through the Collaborator problem-solving approach.

When you develop a plan together and there is partial or no interest, let go of the notion that a signed plan means your child will follow though. This unrealistic expectation leads to parents telling their kids that they can't trust them and that they're irresponsible. These words hurt your children and lead to wall building to protect their injured hearts and self-esteem. Instead, meet your children where they are. Start the problem-solving process with the Collaborator Role and then follow up with the Director Role to guarantee success. The more you respectfully guide your children toward success, the better they will feel about themselves and you.

34.
Why "Why?" Doesn't Work and Other Unhelpful Questions

"Why did you hit your brother?"

"Well, Mom, I'm feeling jealous that you've been spending so much time with him since he was born. I feel neglected, and I resent you, so I take out my hurt feelings on him. I'd be happier if you didn't have him. Aren't I enough?"

Have you ever received a well-thought-out answer like this to your interrogating "why" question? Not likely. It's pretty ridiculous when you think about how many questions we ask our kids that we know they can't answer. The effect of these often accusatory questions is that the child senses our disapproval and feels shamed and humiliated. Their hurt feelings do not lead to open dialogue and problem solving together.

Here are some additional examples of common ineffective questions:

"Why did you do that?"

"Why didn't you...?"

"How many times do I have to tell you?"

"When will you learn to think before you act?"

"How come you're so mean, rude, selfish, etc...?"

Children typically respond to these types of accusatory questions with either, "I don't know," hurtful back talk, or humiliated silence followed by revenge or rebellion at a later time. The child's response depends on the depth of their hurt, their age, and their temperament. Asking a child self-reflective questions without an opportunity to express feelings and thoughts doesn't work because the child hasn't had any time to analyze the problem. You would be amazed at how a child as young as five can think about their thoughts and feelings and make conclusions in the presence of an accepting and supportive listener. You can learn how to be the type of listener your kids come to for support and help. They will feel so loved and accepted by you that their hearts will open more to your requests for support and cooperation in return.

If you have a deep urge to express your own feelings, it's better to express them honestly rather than blame your children for their imperfections. Your tone of voice will communicate concern and a desire to understand and improve the situation. Your goal is to move toward solving the challenge rather than making your kids feel bad in the hopes of effecting change.

Here are some examples of supportive problem-solving statements:

"I wish I understood better what's going on with you. I'd like to listen to you."

"I'm wondering what kept you from turning in your homework after you finished it."

"I wish the two of you could get along better. Let's see what we can do about this."

"I need to understand what's going on in your brain so I can be more helpful and a better parent."

To solve your "why," "how," and "when" questions, start by analyzing what your parenting role should be for each problem: Director, Collaborator, or Supporter/Confidant. This will determine whether you, both you and your child, or your child alone will choose the final solution to try.

Then, engage in self-questioning at a calm time. Working with a supportive adult listening partner is the best way to find your answers to the following questions:

- *Why did my child do that? What goals were being met?*

- *Why didn't my child do what I asked?*

- *Why do I have to keep repeating myself? What's wrong with my approach?"*

- *What is my child's developmental maturity stage?*

- *Am I being patient and understanding and not expecting too much?*

- *Is my child feeling hurt and wanting to hurt in return?*

- *What thoughts are being triggered within me that are making it impossible to stay present and connected?*

If you choose to have a problem-solving session with your child, the following statements are more effective than "why" questions in stimulating closeness, generating discussion, and finding solutions:

"Let's discuss how I can say things so you will respond positively. I don't want to be a nag."

"I see that you're struggling with angry emotions and lashing out. I think you'd feel better about yourself if you didn't hit. Let's talk about what to do instead of hitting."

"Everyone struggles with challenges at different times. I can see that you're struggling now. Let's talk about how I can help you be more successful so you'll feel better about yourself."

When you feel stuck, find a nonjudgmental support person who can review these self-reflective questions listed above with you. Your self-reflective Ally perspective will open your heart and mind. Then, you can have more emotionally connected and productive problem-solving discussions with your children as well as adults.

35.
Family Meetings Build Cooperation and Family Unity

When you hold regular family meetings, you establish family values of connection, unity, mutual respect, support, and creative problem solving. If weekly meetings are too much, then set aside time to meet every two weeks. As a result of your sustained efforts, you will build a family in which problems are discussed, each person feels heard, and adventures are planned because you made family meetings a high priority.

In my family, I insisted on family meetings even though my daughter often resisted and my husband wasn't focused on them. Since we followed Michael Popkin's guideline of giving allowance at the end of the family meeting, my daughter always attended. This incentive, which didn't involve nagging her, worked well because we didn't connect her allowance to her behavior. Rather, we used allowance for teaching money management, which was one of the skills we would talk about during our family meetings. Keeping your children engaged in the family meeting process is important. Make sure to discuss pleasant topics along with unpleasant topics so that having a family meeting isn't simply another name for your children being in trouble.

As a result of nine years of family meetings, I have a treasure trove of handwritten meeting notes that serve as a memoir of our family life. During our meetings, we covered topics such as chores, vacations, time management, TV viewing, school, sports, dance classes, pet care, family purchases, cell phones, boys, party rules, friends, use of allowance, and finally, my daughter getting a restaurant hostess job at age 15. When you insist on family meetings despite the many obstacles life throws your way, you create a family that values and treasures one another.

Following is a framework for starting your own family meetings.

General Guidelines for Effective and Joyful Family Meetings

- Before each meeting, post a sheet of paper in a common area of your home for family members to write down what they want to talk about during the meeting. A family meeting is not a time for parents to tell kids what they're doing wrong and need to change. It's a time for family members to encourage each other and work together to meet needs. Children often resist the family meeting because they think it's only a time when parents tell them they need to change rather than a time that they will be heard.

- Encourage problem solving during your meetings. Use the Joint-Problem-Solving Process as a blueprint for your discussions.

- Talk about positive ideas as well as what needs to change. Plan an outing.

- Make your family meetings fun. Rotate who will come up with a funny joke or activity for each meeting.

- If appropriate, give allowance at the end of the family meeting to encourage participation. You can tell your kids, "You will receive your allowance at the end of the meeting."

- Keep a log of meeting notes to refer to at each meeting.

- Set a time limit. Whatever doesn't get addressed within that time frame is put on the agenda for the next meeting.

- Try to set a consistent day and time for family meetings even though obstacles will arise.

- Tell your family members how important their opinions are.

- Consider having your kids make a talking stick, a Native American tradition, or another item that will be held by the speaker. This visual cue of whose time it is to speak will teach children how to wait until their turn and reduce interruptions.

Leadership Roles

These roles rotate at each meeting depending on your child's maturity level. Keep in mind that, hopefully, you will continue your family meetings for years to come, so if your child isn't ready for a leadership role yet, they will be in the future as they continue to learn from you.

The Chairperson keeps the discussion on track and ensures that everyone's opinions are heard.

The Secretary takes notes during the meeting. Depending on their interest level and age, the secretary may also write the official minutes after the meeting. In my family, we never wrote minutes, but you may have a child who likes to do so. At the next meeting, the secretary for that meeting reads the previous meeting's notes to review your past decisions and follow up on how you did.

Family Meeting Agenda

1. Compliments: Encourage appreciative statements about one another.

2. Minutes: Review minutes from the previous meeting.

3. Old Business/New Business: Address topics not covered during the previous meeting, followed by new topics.

4. Allowances: If appropriate, give allowances. Allowances are an encouragement to attend family meetings.

5. Treat or Family Activity: End each meeting on a positive note.

Ground Rules for Conducting Problem-Solving Discussions

- Every person has an equal voice.

- Everyone may say what they think and feel about each issue.

- Use only respectful language.

- Decisions are made by consensus, if it is a joint problem to solve.

- All decisions are in effect until the next meeting date or date otherwise specified.

- Some decisions are reserved for parents to make.

These guidelines are suggestions, so change them as needed. However, keep the family meeting as a time when everyone practices not blocking communication and listening without judgment. That way, each person feels safe and shares. After sharing, teach your children how to disagree without demeaning each other. With gentle reminders, the ability to be open-minded and respectful will grow. Most of all, enjoy the special time you have carved out of your busy schedules to be together as a family.

36.
The Collaborator Parenting Role:
Managing Sibling Conflicts

Each sibling conflict gives us an opportunity to teach children valuable problem-solving skills. Rather than acting as the judge, as if you own the problem, realize that it is a joint problem because the kids and the adults both want the problem solved. You are tired of the bickering, and you want your kids to be loving toward one another. At the same time, your kids want their annoying sibling stopped. They may look like they enjoy fighting because they do it so often. In reality, though, they are frustrated because they're trying to problem solve with limited skills.

Rather than tell them to figure it out on their own, which they obviously can't do, approach sibling conflicts as teachable moments. When you do, you create a home atmosphere in which everyone works together for the betterment of the family.

During the problem-solving process, the Ally parent thinks, *How am I going to teach my kids to become more responsible for their behavior so they will get along better?* As you teach your children the steps of the problem-solving process, they will gradually handle conflicts more maturely with less unproductive fighting. The process can feel daunting because problem solving takes time, requires effective communication skills, and depends on your child's age. Rest assured that the time you invest in teaching problem solving will be less than you would spend trying to solve problems for your children.

A common parental trap during sibling conflicts is listening to a child's complaints and judging who is innocent and who is guilty according to their testimony. Usually, your child runs to you saying something like, "Mommy, Mommy, Brian hit me." Your protective instincts kick in, and the supposed perpetrator is found guilty and punished. Once you respond this way, your kids learn how to get you on their side. If they can make you the judge who scolds the other sibling rather than the Collaborator who teaches them both how to be responsible for the conflict, your complaining child feels like a winner and doesn't have to change. Your child has just learned to blame others for his problems.

The Joint-Problem-Solving Process is a crucial life skill designed to teach children that everyone takes responsibility for finding solutions together because no one person is at fault. Not only will understanding this relationship rule make your interactions with your children healthier, but it will also prepare them for long-term adult relationships.

Most siblings have recurring conflicts, such as the younger sibling annoying the older one or the older sibling shutting out the younger one. Their responses are triggered by goals they are trying to achieve. I suggest you read Chapter 16 titled, *Why Children Do What They Do – It's Not About You*, in Section 3, to better understand the purpose of fighting so you can remain less emotionally triggered and therefore better equipped to teach the problem-solving process.

The Collaborator Problem-Solving Process with Siblings

Use Chapter 32, *Finding Solutions Together: The Collaborator Role*, in this section as a companion chapter to understand the basic steps for solving all joint problems. The Joint-Problem-Solving Process is as follows:

1. Stop blocking communication

2. Listen openly to feelings

3. Discuss and evaluate ideas

4. Make a plan together

5. Follow up to determine success and try another idea, if needed.

Refer to Section 2, Creating Open Communication, to learn how to work through steps one and two.

The third step is to discuss and evaluate ideas. Before you begin, set clear guidelines for respectful and effective problem solving. The first guideline is to teach how to listen without interrupting. To visually designate whose turn it is, the speaker could hold an item such as a "talking stick," which is a Native American tradition, or set a timer for uninterrupted talking time. A second guideline may be that it is not permitted to verbally attack and blame each other, such as, "Mark always picks on me," because it shuts down communication. Instead, encourage feelings and descriptions of what happened, such as, "I don't like it when Mark won't let me use the computer when it's my turn. He just teases me."

During the discussion, create a safe and accepting environment by continuing to avoid communication blocks and listen with empathy to each child. Each person should share their emotions and thoughts about the conflicts. Before kids can think rationally and produce possible solutions, they need to feel heard and acknowledged. You can repeat what they have said, interpret the feelings behind their words and seek agreement, or simply say, "I see." Choose language that keeps your child talking.

Your description of how the problem impacts you is just as important. You may share, "I feel hurt and upset when you fight. I want to help everyone find a better way to get along so that our house is happier. I'm going to stop judging who is right and who is wrong. Instead, I will tell you what I see happening." Do not tell them, "You should know how to get along with each other." They don't and it's your job to teach them how.

While solutions are being generated by everyone, keep the "listen without interrupting" rule in force. When interruptions happen, give a gentle reminder, such as, "It's your brother's turn. Please give him a chance to finish, and then you will have your turn." Ask one of the kids to write down the suggestions so they feel involved in the process. Brainstorm many solutions first before evaluating them.

It's challenging to go through the entire five step process in one sitting. You may only get through brainstorming ideas before everyone is ready to stop. You can say, "I think we've done enough for now. We have a list of ideas. We'll talk again at (a set time) and find one solution to try first. Thank you for sharing. We understand each other better now."

In step four, you make the plan together. As you evaluate each idea, be careful not to direct the discussion toward your solution. Even if you believe yours is the "best" solution, kids need to feel like it's their solution in order for them to follow the plan. Teens, in particular, will be unlikely to choose a solution when it's your plan. As a parent, you do have the power to veto any ideas that break family rules, are unfair, or that you're unwilling to enforce. Since the primary conflict is between the siblings, let them choose the initial plan, as long as you also approve of that plan.

For example, during the discussion, you may find out that the younger sibling feels ignored by the older one and that's why they get into her things. This may be leading to the older sibling getting angry and pulling away more. When you understand the goals of the behavior, the discussion could sound like this:

Parent: "It looks like your little sister needs to feel connected and important to you. I agree that bugging you is not a good way to get your attention because it only makes you mad. While she is working on not getting into your things, what are ideas of what you could do to make her feel more important to you?"

Older sibling: "I could set the timer, like we do during our discussion, for 10 minutes and just play with her. Then, I would expect her to leave me alone."

Parent: "That's one idea. What might be another possibility?"

Older sibling: "I could get a lock on my door so she can't come in."

Parent: "That's a second idea."

You may be thinking that your child would say, "I don't know." This is a typical response when kids haven't had time to express the feelings that are causing them to get stuck. When they express their emotions and ideas and you carefully listen to them without judgment, they will be willing and able to be creative and thoughtful.

Returning to the example above, after ideas are shared, review each one asking, "How would you feel doing that? What would the result be of doing that?" If the older child doesn't have too much hurt and resentment built up toward the younger one, she will be able to acknowledge that it would be best to spend a short period of time with her sister each day rather than lock her out.

Then, you would ask for ideas from the younger sibling about what she could do differently and what she thinks about her older sibling's idea. Try this process with children as young as three. If they are mature enough, they will amaze you with how aware they are about feelings and what is fair.

During the problem-solving process, you are a Collaborator because the problem at hand is one that everyone wants solved. Therefore, it's essential that you agree on the final decision because you will be supervising the follow-through in the Director Role.

When the desired solution is selected, write it down, have everyone sign it, and post it in a visible place. Avoid threats such as stating what will happen if the kids don't stick to the agreement. Your predetermined consequence sets the tone of expected failure, rather than success. Instead say, "We'll check back in on ____, and if this solution isn't working, we'll discuss another idea. Does everyone understand and agree?" Depending on how often the conflicts happen, you may give them a time frame from two days to one week to try the chosen plan before reviewing its effectiveness.

During the practice time, your job is to redirect them to the plan when they get off-track and start fighting again, which they probably will. Don't nag, yell, or give up on them. Change takes time. Try saying, "Let's review the plan that you decided to try. It's hard for everyone to change bad habits like fighting and hitting."

Step five involves meeting at a designated time to follow up on how the plan is going. Is there less arguing? Do they see improvement? Do they want to keep trying, or do they need to try another idea? It's important for children to learn that we don't always make the best choice the first time and that's okay. This is a learning process.

During the follow-up discussion, if the current plan isn't working, you could say, "It looks like you're having a hard time playing with your sister." If the older sibling is playing and the younger one is still bothering her, you could say, "It looks like even though your sister is playing with you, you're still bugging her." Continue to practice not blocking communication and listening openly to discover what's going on. Then, you can discuss another solution and develop a new plan.

Children need guidance to find solutions because their reasoning brains aren't fully developed and won't be until ages 25 to 29. This collaborative problem-solving process teaches your kids how to listen to each other respectfully, understand another person's perspective, not always get their own way, and that they are capable of solving problems. A big part of your job as a parent is to teach this invaluable life skill of problem solving. You will be amazed at how practicing this loving and beautiful process creates bonds of deep trust and connection for a lifetime.

37.
Choose Supportive Problem Solving Rather Than Directing

Imagine this scenario. Your son or daughter comes home from school visibly upset. You've already learned how to connect with your child by listening empathetically rather than interrogating, commanding, or using other communication blocks. You have established trust, and you know your son or daughter wants to find a solution to a problem that is theirs to solve.

Picture yourself and your child standing at the bottom of a mountain. At the top of the mountain is a good first solution to the problem at hand. In order to be an effective resource for your child's problem-solving process, ask yourself, *Which road will be most successful in reaching the top of the mountain together?* You can try the treacherous Director road, or you can choose the winding Supporter road.

If you are inexperienced at problem solving with your children, you will probably choose the Director road because it's familiar. This road, however, blocks the opportunity to teach your child the problem-solving process he needs to master to become a responsible adult.

Your choice of the Director road would likely be based on your immediate goals to:

- Lessen your child's suffering

- Lessen your own suffering that comes from watching your child suffer

- Find a solution that will quickly resolve the problem because you're out of time

- Tell your child what to do because you assume she can't figure it out on her own

When you choose the Director road, you are trying to control the situation. Time constraints, situational pressures, and safety concerns are common factors in choosing this controlling approach. When you don't take the time to teach kids how to find their own solutions, they remain irresponsible, and you complain about it. You create the exact opposite of what you want.

The Supporter road takes more time in the beginning, yet the camaraderie you will feel with your kids is well worth the effort. When choosing the Supporter problem-solving role, it is important to understand the objectives and underlying beliefs of this approach. In so doing, you train your brain to see conflicts as opportunities to:

- Teach the problem-solving process, not only to solve the current issue, but also as an important life skill

- Develop closer relationships with your children because they will trust and rely on you during difficulties

- Strengthen your children's abilities to handle adversity and develop self-confidence

- Gain wisdom about emotional intelligence and how to help others when they're struggling

Even though the quick-solution Director route seems faster, it's actually slower because it's filled with strong resistance from your child. Most kids (and adults) don't like to be controlled and don't respond well to your attempts to drive the conversation. You will realize that you've chosen the Director road when your child responds to your attempts to find a solution by saying:

"I don't know."

"You don't understand."

"Leave me alone."

"No. That idea is stupid."

"I don't know," is a common response when parents ask, "What are you going to do?" Since the child hasn't gone through the process of sharing emotions, brainstorming and evaluating ideas, and deciding on a first choice, he can't possibly know what to do. You've skipped the entire problem-solving process, jumped ahead, and requested the final decision prematurely.

Telling your child "I know what you should do" can be just as dangerous. This Director remark sends your child the message that he can't find a solution so you have to figure it out for him. Since interrogating and giving unwanted advice can feel hurtful to your child, communication usually shuts down, leaving everyone feeling frustrated, not valued, and discouraged.

Take time to learn the Supporter problem-solving process:

1. Avoid communication blocks

2. Listen openly

3. Discuss ideas and choose a solution

4. Check in later

Some children like to discuss problems thoroughly with parents and get their input. Try not to influence your child's final decision because if it doesn't work out, they will blame you. If you offer your idea as the best one, it's still your idea, even if they agree with you. It's better to say "I'm not sure what you should do," and continue discussing the possibilities rather than answer the child's question, "What do you think I should do?"

While some children like discussing problems thoroughly with parents and getting their input, other children want you to listen with empathy as they share their struggles. They will figure out what to do later, on their own. Simply beginning the problem-solving process by listening with empathy will release enough tension for their logical brain to engage. You can let them know that you are available later if they want to talk about their challenge.

When you focus on supporting your child's decision-making process, you communicate confidence in their ability to successfully manage life. You develop a family that faces problems with courage and confidence rather than fear and uncertainty.

38.
How to Be Your Child's Trusted Supporter and Confidant

Knowing how to successfully support your struggling child is an invaluable skill that you'll use throughout your lifetime. Regardless of your child's age, when you master the roles of Supporter and Confidant, your children will come to you when they're under duress or making decisions. I believe we can build the greatest connections, sense of security, and thus joy with our children during their difficult times. So, embrace your child's growth opportunities and be their Supporter, with the confidence of knowing that you're strengthening your family's foundation forever.

Parents often confuse opportunities to be the Collaborator and solve problems together with opportunities to be the Supporter or Confidant and let their child decide on a solution. As a guideline, you should choose the Supporter or Confidant Role when:

- Your child is the one who wants to find a solution, and the problem at hand directly affects only them

- The decision does not involve family rules, values, health, or safety

- With your support, your child is able to find a solution, based on their age and maturity

It's essential to give your children increased decision-making opportunities as they mature so that they can experience success and failure before leaving home. If you overprotect your children by doing too much for them, rescuing them, or making excuses for them, you weaken them and reduce their ability to live successful lives. If this is your tendency, learn how to manage your own fears and lack of confidence in your child as these will keep you from being an effective Supporter.

The Supporter Parenting Role is a four-step problem-solving process. Choose this role when your child wants to discuss possible solutions with you and come to a decision with your encouragement. Your child will select a solution naturally while pondering ideas with you or afterwards.

Some children don't want to discuss their possible solutions with you. They only want you to listen to them, like a confidant, rather than you sharing your ideas or discussing theirs. So, in the Confidant Role, you first stop blocking communication and then listen openly so your child can process their thoughts and feelings with you. That's it. If you start suggesting ideas or asking them what they are thinking and they get irritated with you and stop sharing, then you have gone too far. Stop and say, "I'm sorry. You just want me to listen right now." Realize that your listening gives your child a very important opportunity to think aloud and process their thoughts, which will lead to improved decision making.

There's a good chance that your child will share with you later what they decided because they trust that you won't tell them they're wrong. In both the Supporter and Confidant Roles, your presence and nonjudgmental listening give your child's brain a much needed opportunity to process, evaluate, and take action with greater clarity and confidence.

The Supporter Problem-Solving Process

Step 1: Stop Blocking Communication

In an attempt to "help," adults often say things that shut down or block communication, which can lead to anger and hurt for everyone. A communication block, as defined by Michael Popkin, PhD, is any remark or attitude on the part of the listener that injures the speaker's self-esteem enough to break communication. You will feel an invisible wall go up instantly when this happens.

Examples of communication blocks are commanding, giving unwanted advice, placating, interrogating, distracting, psychologizing, sarcasm, moralizing, being a know-it-all, me-tooism, and yelling. Your awareness of how your comments impact others' willingness to talk will improve your communication in many situations, both within and outside of the family. For details on how to avoid communication blocks, study Chapter 10 in Section 2, *Awareness of Communication Blocks Is the First Step.*

Step 2: Listen Openly

This crucial step of the problem-solving process develops your empathy and a deeper level of connection and influence between yourself and your child. Children cannot discuss ideas logically when in an emotional state. They will refuse to "move on" and think logically until you've listened respectfully and responded with empathy and nonjudgment toward their thoughts and feelings. For details on how to listen openly and with empathy, study these chapters in Section 2, *The Emotional Support Process Connects You to Your Child*, *Empathy Improves Connection and Communication*, and *Parent Success Stories of Using Empathetic Responses*.

Be careful to avoid pushing your child to discuss solutions before they're ready. When you do, this means that you're more concerned with finding a solution than teaching your child how to make their own decisions. If you push your child, they will end up resisting you, likely get angry at you, and stop talking with you, which you don't want. Remember that being patient and tuning into your child's own process creates time for better self-understanding, which will lead to improved problem solving in Step 3 of the process. Delay the evaluation of ideas until Step 3.

Step 3: Discuss Ideas and Let Your Child Choose a Solution

In the Supporter Parenting Role, you brainstorm ideas together, evaluate possible outcomes together, and then your child decides which solution to try first. This process gives your child an opportunity to learn from their successes and failures. Practice self-restraint, and do not tell your child what to do.

Keep the following thoughts in mind while discussing ideas together:

- *One of the greatest life skills I can teach my child is how to face problems head-on and solve them, rather than being afraid and defeated by them.*

- *I need to give my child permission to choose their own solution so that they will learn how to take responsibility for their actions, rather than blame others. This is my child's problem to solve with my support.*

- *Because we learn from our mistakes, I will teach my child that if the first solution doesn't work, try another solution.*

- *My child has their own path to follow, so I don't have the right to tell them what to do.*

Examples of problem-solving conversations:

"Let's think about some possible things you could do to solve this problem."

"It's hard to know what to do, and I don't know what you'll decide in the end."

"I'd like to help you think about it."

"What's one possible solution? What do you think would happen if you did that?"

"What's another possible idea?"

"I have an idea. Would you like to hear it?"

"There's no right answer, so we can come up with many possibilities. "

"Of the ideas you've come up with, which one would you like to try first?"

Step 4: Check in Later

Your check-in conversation can be as casual as, "How did it go with solving the problem we talked about?" Perhaps it went well, and you will celebrate together. If, during your problem-solving discussion, it was made clear that the first choice doesn't always work out, then any disappointment will be easier to share.

If your child hasn't acted yet, it may be helpful to repeat Step 2 of the problem-solving process by allowing time to listen openly to the feelings and thoughts that have been keeping them from moving forward. Perhaps their decision is too scary, and they need additional encouragement to reassure them that they can handle whatever happens.

Your child may also need to hear that not taking action is as valid a choice as taking action, or maybe they want to try another idea. Listening and having confidence in their maturing brain as they struggle will give them self-confidence as well. Your child needs to know that you're not expecting perfection and that you aren't judging them.

Continue to look for opportunities to solve problems together rather than tell your kids what to do. Reflect on problem ownership in order to select the proper parenting role for each situation. Problem solving develops self-esteem, so allow many opportunities to struggle and win together.

39.
The Supporter Parenting Role:
The "Boredom Problem"

Example:

Child: "I'm bored. There's nothing to do."

Potential parent responses:

"What do you mean you're bored and there's nothing to do? You can help me fold the laundry, play with your sister, or read."

"I buy you all of these toys, and you just ignore them."

"When I was your age, I played outside. You should do that."

These parent responses are examples of communication blocks, and they usually upset the child because the parent is trying to fix a problem that isn't theirs to fix. Your child is making a complaint and needs to find their own solution. Therefore, when you respond sarcastically, give advice, moralize, or engage in me-tooism, they feel hurt rather than helped. Your unintended message is that they are not capable of figuring out what to do on their own. This message conveys the exact opposite of what you want, i.e., your child to figure out how to not be bored.

As parents, we often have a difficult time hearing the "boredom complaint" because it triggers our own upset feelings when our child is unhappy. These feelings can come from believing we're bad parents or remembering childhood times when we felt hurt. As a result of our pain, we try to fix the source of our unhappiness in the moment, our child. Therefore, instead of helping our child, we block communication. When our child then rejects our help, we feel hurt and may get angry. This pattern of interaction continues in a vicious cycle until we learn to approach the problem differently.

Shifting how you handle the "boredom problem" starts with asking yourself who owns the problem and who is requesting to find a solution. Your child wants to not be bored, and no rules are broken, so your child is responsible for finding the solution. When you tell your kids what to do, you are assuming the Director Role. Since the problem is theirs to solve, this situation calls for you to choose the problem-solving Supporter Role to guide your kids toward a good solution of their choice. Don't miss out on this fantastic opportunity to teach problem-solving skills!

Your Supporter/Confidant Role consists of four problem-solving steps. They are:

1. Stop blocking communication

2. Listen openly

3. Discuss ideas and let your child choose a solution

4. Check in later

Read the previous chapter, *How to Be Your Child's Trusted Supporter and Confidant*, for a full description of the four steps.

The first step is to stop blocking communication. The second step, listen openly, can be particularly challenging with the boredom problem because of the critical thoughts about your child that usually creep in. Here are some empathetic statements to try so your child can keep venting until they can think logically and come up with some play ideas. Remember, that you create this supportive space when you respond with tentative comments about your child's experience. Notice that the following examples are not questions, but statements that can be refuted by your child. You aren't trying to be right, just supportive because your child doesn't need you to fix his problem.

"Not knowing what to do is frustrating."

"I guess nothing seems fun right now."

"You sound lonely."

"You're having a hard time right now."

"It seems like you might not be interested in the same things any more."

Try out these suggestions and create your own statements that allow space and time for your child to release her emotions. After each empathetic statement, be quiet in order to gently loosen your child's stuck feelings so they can flow out of the frazzled limbic system, the emotional system within the brain. Your child may need several empathetic responses from you before she is ready to solve the problem logically.

After listening to venting, venture into the third step of problem solving, which involves the logical brain known as the prefrontal cortex. Your attitude must be, *This is my child's problem to solve, so he will make the final decision. I'm not going to sway him in any direction because that could feel manipulative. I'll help evaluate our suggestions. This is a chance for him to practice problem solving with my support. It will also build our relationship.* Here is an abbreviated example of the four-step problem-solving process where you are a Supporter:

Step 1: Avoid Blocking Communication

Step 2: Listen with Empathy

Child: "I'm bored. There's nothing to do."

Parent: "That's too bad." (Don't use blocks. Just use empathy.)

Child: "There's no one to play with, and there's nothing to do."

Parent: "You sound stuck. I wonder what you'll find to do."

Child: "Everyone is busy." (Be careful to not disagree with this exaggeration. Your child is venting now.)

Parent: "That's hard."

Child: "I wish I had someone to play with."

Parent: "That would be nice."

Step 3: Discuss Ideas and Let Your Child Choose a Solution

Parent: "We could come up with some ideas together, if that would be helpful."

Child: "Okay."

Parent: "How about you start with an idea."

Child: "I don't know. I guess I could call Matt."

Parent: "You could. Another idea is to build one of your models."

Child: "I'd rather do something with my friends."

Parent: "That's good to know. It sounds like Matt would be a good place to start."

Child: "I'll call him now."

Parent: "I'd be okay with either playing here or at his house. Let me know what he says, and then we'll go from there."

Step 4: Check In Later

Parent: "So, I'm wondering if you made a decision of what to do this afternoon."

Child: "Matt can't come over so I might call Jeff."

Parent: "Well, it sounds like you're figuring it out."

Confidant Role: If your child only wants to vent and doesn't want to discuss ideas with you, then you stop after making empathetic statements in Step 2. You might end with saying, "I'm sure you'll figure it out. Let me know if you need my help."

Patience, self-awareness, and a nonjudgmental attitude are necessary qualities in the Supporter/Confidant Role as you guide children on the path to successfully solving problems. As you develop these qualities, you will boost your child's development of their logical prefrontal cortex and develop a tighter bond and support system between family members.

40.
Parent Success Stories About Solving Problems

Mom and Dad Create Family Unity with Teenage Son

My husband and I received parenting support from Cynthia for 1½ years with wonderful results. We attended one of Cynthia's parenting seminars because we had been suffering through four years of an intense relationship with our teenage son who was 16 years old at the time. We were raised in China and believed we should have control over our son. He didn't agree, so he stopped sharing with us.

Our goal was to improve our communication with our son. Cynthia taught us about communication blocks and how to decide whether you or your teenager has ownership for solving a problem. "Communication blocks?" We had never heard of them. We thought the problem was that our son didn't listen to us, that he had the problem and needed to change, not us. Cynthia told us that if we changed, our son would change.

We hired Cynthia as our private parenting coach. After meeting with her for just two hours, we were impressed with how she was able to analyze our situation and point out what we were doing that caused our problem.

Cynthia encouraged us to talk with our son about communication blocks and ask for his opinion about them. We told him that we were working on changing. The first step was to stop giving him advice that he wasn't even listening to. We also learned how to discuss important issues with him without judgment. Through doing so, he felt our respect for his own thoughts and feelings. Because we would sit back and describe the situation, he didn't feel pushed by us and was, therefore, more open to our thoughts.

For example, we made him the decision maker about which college to attend. We said, "This decision is yours to make."

We listened to his thoughts about each college we visited, and if he didn't like it, it was off the list, regardless of our opinion. Before working with Cynthia, we would have been very controlling and told him where to apply. We thought that was how to make sure he would be happy. We found out that this controlling approach only made him closed down and unhappy with us.

Over the past 1½ years of individualized parenting education, Cynthia helped us remove our communication blocks step by step, learn the proper parenting role for each problem, accept our son's opinions, and create a "happy hour" during which we give him total attention.

Now, our relationship is much more relaxed, trusting, and happy. Because of these changes, our son is also happier, more confident, and has expanded his circle of friends. He recently said to us, "You are much better than before." Cynthia, you are very important to our family, and we greatly appreciate what you have done for us.

Mom Creates a Successful Homework Plan with Son

I've been receiving private parenting coaching from Cynthia, and I needed help with my 7-year-old's son's resistance to doing homework.

Because I didn't think he was getting enough practice in school, I enrolled my son in additional tutoring. I had to constantly push him to do his homework as well as his tutoring work. He'd say, "Ok, I'll do it. I'll do it." I would keep pushing, and he would get upset, cry, scream, and say, "I hate tutoring."

Cynthia helped me realize that I was taking on my son's homework as if it were totally my issue rather than mine and his.

She taught me how to talk with my son about homework being a joint problem to solve together since he is too young to figure out when to do it and to be committed to doing it on his own.

Cynthia suggested that my son and I develop a homework plan together.

My son knows that I'm seeking parenting coaching, so I had a problem-solving discussion with him. Here is how our conversation went:

Mom: "Remember how I'm getting help with parenting? Well, I talked to my coach about the homework battles we're having. She gave me some homework to do, and I need your help with it. She suggested that we come up with a homework plan together. I shouldn't be getting so angry and frustrated about you not doing your homework, and you should be taking more ownership for doing your homework. We'll figure out how you can take part in developing your homework plan so that you'll know what you're supposed to be doing."

Son: "Great, Mom. Now I can help you with your homework like you help me with mine."

Mom: "Yes. So, tell me, how do you feel about homework?"

Son: "Sometimes, I don't like it, especially the extra tutoring work I have to do."

Mom: "What do think about the tutoring work?"

Son: "I don't like it most of the time."

Mom: "Why?"

Son: "Because it's hard, and it's a higher level for me. I get frustrated. Sometimes, I don't like the homework from school because it's harder now."

Mom: "You find the homework hard, and that's the part you don't like?"

Son: "Yes."

Mom: "So, when it's hard, does that make you feel like you're dumb? Does it frustrate you?"

Son: "Well, no, not really. Most of the time, I don't feel like I'm dumb."

Mom: "So, tell me what you really think. What do you think about taking tutoring away?"

Son: "I'm not sure. That's a really hard question. Well, my tutoring work is hard in the beginning. It gets to newer levels, and it's way beyond what I know. But, there are good parts, too. Since I've been doing the extra reading comprehension work in my tutoring, I found a reading test in school easy."

Mom: "Yeah! The purpose is to make school easier. Does the tutoring help you feel confident about yourself in school?"

Son: "I feel really good in school this year because I'm ahead of everyone. Last year, I could hardly do addition. I didn't feel good about myself then."

Mom: "What do you think, then, about continuing the tutoring?"

Son: "Yeah, I don't think I want to stop my tutoring. I think I want to keep going."

Mom: "Ok, we can continue. If you find it difficult, we can talk to the teacher and cut down from 10 pages to 5 pages, keep you on a certain level longer, or go slower. Let me know when it gets too difficult so we can talk to the teacher."

Mom: "Ok, let's make a homework plan. When is the best time to do homework?"

Son: "I need time to have a snack first when I come home."

Mom: "Do you need time to do anything else?"

Son: "Yeah, maybe to play or read to help me relax."

We decided to use the term "unwind time," which my son really liked. We set aside 30 minutes of "unwind time" after school each day, 30 minutes to do whatever he wants — snack, read, and/or play.

I identified a potential problem of my son reading for 30 minutes then wanting to eat, and I brought this up to him. He decided on 15 minutes for eating and 15 minutes for fun. He will be responsible for setting a timer. After 30 minutes, he will do his homework first, which should take about 20 minutes. Then, he will do his tutoring work, which should take no more than an hour.

My son suggested a minor change when he has special days. "The plan has to change on the days I have activities," he said.

For example, today he told me that he is going to come home and eat while doing his homework since he has a special activity. He decided that after homework, he'll do his activity, come home, and then do his tutoring work so he can go to his friend's house to watch the basketball game.

My son was looking forward to taking on responsibility for following his homework plan. We both signed the agreement and posted it.

This morning, he woke up excited and said, "Mom, I'm so happy that I have a plan today about my homework."

Then, Cynthia reminded me to set up a check-in date. I'm worried that my son won't keep following our plan. She explained that everyone needs to be recharged when they make a determination. Rather than getting mad at him if he starts to slip and feeling like I have to start nagging, have a check-in session. Discuss again how it's going and remind him how much better he feels when he takes responsibility rather than having me take over and nag him.

I am so excited to be viewing homework as a joint problem to solve together with my son and to be using my collaborative parenting role skills so I won't feel taken advantage of and used. Thank you so much, Cynthia.

Added Note from Cynthia: Because children often don't stay excited about doing homework, this mom also used the Director Role After-Then Strategy to ensure follow-through.

A United Parenting Plan Creates Family Harmony

My wife and I contacted Cynthia for help with three issues:

1. How to deal with our very physical son

2. Wanting to come together more on our parenting approach

3. Stopping the fighting between our two sons

Over the past two months, we have made great progress. Thanks to Cynthia's advice, our parenting approach has become more cohesive, as we talk about and work through challenges together.

We always leave her office with a plan for what to work on.

My wife sees it like tackling a whole movie by working on snapshots of what's happening in the moment. Changing each moment is how the entire movie changes.

We see our shortcomings and how to compensate for one another more clearly.

We've been working more as a team as we support each other's attempts at changing rather than criticizing each other. I've been working specifically on what to say when each recurring problem arises, such as jumping on the couch.

We're having more family discussions about issues and setting guidelines rather than trying to stop "bad" behavior by responding emotionally in the moment.

We're learning how to proactively plan for redirecting potential problems. We value greatly the time we spend with Cynthia because of her deep understanding, knowledge, and encouragement.

Our family has less conflict and more harmony as we practice the skills Cynthia is teaching us.

Teens Need Structure to Get Things Done

I'm a mom of three children.

My two teenage girls share a bathroom, and I want them to be responsible for cleaning it. I had been taking a hands-off approach until it got so bad that I would tell them loudly that I couldn't stand it anymore and they had to clean it. I knew they liked it when the bathroom was clean, yet left to their own devices, they would wait until I couldn't stand it anymore. My husband and I talked to Cynthia about this problem.

First, we needed to approach it as a joint problem because I wanted the bathroom to be cleaned, just as my daughters did. I was embarrassed when friends came over and saw the awful bathroom. This meant that I couldn't leave it up to them as I had been. I realized that I wanted the bathroom cleaned twice a month, and Cynthia, my husband, and I decided that Saturdays were best.

Here is how I approached my daughters. I told them that I needed their help, that the bathroom needed to be cleaned regularly because it matters to me. I started by getting their input. I asked them about their strategy for sharing the cleaning and how that was working. They decided on the distribution of chores. Some places were hard to clean, such as the ceiling, so I helped a little. At one point, one of my daughters wanted a ride somewhere, so I used the After-Then approach and said, "I'll drive you after the bathroom is cleaned." She grumbled and said, "This is a fun thing to do on my day off." I didn't respond, even though I was thinking, *This is what we do on our days off.*

Overall, it was a good experience. I took a picture of the clean bathroom and posted it. My daughters know that in two weeks, they will clean it again. I realized that they need me to provide structure to get it done, so I'll provide the structure as long as needed.

Listening to My Nagging Daughter Works Best

I struggle with managing my anger with my very strong-willed 5-year-old daughter.

My daughter is often very demanding and tells me what to do. When I say that I can't do something, she keeps nagging at me and starts to scream and throw a tantrum. She also gets upset if her clothing doesn't feel right. I try to give her alternatives or console her, but things only get worse. I end up becoming very angry with her. I desperately needed help and didn't see how things could change.

Cynthia was recommended to me as a parenting educator who specializes in parental anger and power struggle challenges.

I signed up for her private parenting education program, and right away, I started learning what I was doing that was making the problem worse. First, when giving directions, I kept engaging in arguing back when my daughter resisted an attempt to get her to change. I learned that I had to change my thinking from, *She's the problem and I need to fix her,* to *What can I do differently to get a more positive response from her?* I'm working on stating my expectation, then restating it with even fewer words, if necessary, and not engaging. This approach works so much better.

My big breakthrough came when I could respond to my daughter with empathy when she was upset rather than try to make her stop. Cynthia taught me that any upset child needs to feel heard before they can think clearly. It's very hard to listen, but I tried, with great success.

My daughter was very upset because she didn't want to do her bedtime routine, which includes washing up, brushing her teeth, and reading a book. She was screaming and crying. I can't stand when she acts this way.

Normally, I would either tell her firmly to stop it and try to isolate her to calm her down, or I would just scream back at her, which made both of us feel horrible.

On this occasion, I used Cynthia's advice instead. I controlled my temper and said, "Come here. Let me hold you. Are you sad?"

I was amazed how positively my daughter responded to this empathetic approach. She calmed down much more quickly than she had in the past.

She even opened up and shared that she was upset about school. She said that none of her girlfriends would play with her. I realized that this was the big reason behind her upset. She hadn't shared her true feelings with me before, probably because she didn't feel safe to share when I was always upset with her.

I felt so happy and surprised that she shared her sad feelings with me. I thanked her for talking to me about something so important.

Now, Cynthia is helping me learn how to talk so that my daughter will open up more and I can help her think about possible solutions to her friendship challenges.

Cynthia has taught me to avoid telling my daughter what to do. Instead, I use the Supporter Role Problem-Solving Process and my daughter makes the final decision about what to do. This gives her power over her life, which stops her from trying to have power over me.

Teaching My Kids How to Solve Problems Works

My wife and I have three children, ages 14, 10, and 9. We had participated in some of Cynthia's parenting classes and tried to apply her strategies on our own. We weren't very effective because we couldn't see what we needed to change. Then, we decided to start one-on-one parenting education sessions with Cynthia, and what a huge difference those sessions have made!

Cynthia has taught us valuable problem-solving skills. We now see ourselves more as coaches who help our kids solve problems instead of the judge, jury, and jailer roles we often played in the past. On a recent walk around our neighborhood, our 9- and 10-year-olds started fighting over who got to use the scooter with the "better" handle.

My normal response would have been to put myself in the middle and try to arbitrate or just make a ruling one way or the other. I started down this path and became very frustrated when the kids weren't responding to my ideas.

Just as I was about to put an end to the walk and head home, I decided to give Cynthia's approach a try. I explained that this was a problem that I was going to help my kids solve themselves. Then, I made sure that each kid got a chance to speak, uninterrupted, directly to the other kid, rather than to me as the judge. Once each child had heard the other out, they came up with a fair solution together that was 10 times better than anything I could have imposed on them.

Parents Learning to Trust 16-Year-Old's Judgment

My wife and I were raised in a culture in which parents tell children what to do. The fundamental cultural belief is that children are immature and they don't know how to manage life. Basically, parents know best, and they need to continually direct children.

The result of this approach with our 16-year-old son has not been positive. He doesn't want our advice about studying and now tells us to leave him alone. We don't have the close relationship that both of us would like. We are working with Cynthia to try to improve our communication.

It is very hard for us to change. For example, our son didn't study for the AP and SAT tests like we thought he should. We kept pushing him to study the way we would have studied, and he kept telling us that he knows how much he should study.

We learned that our fear and worry were unfounded when our son earned perfect scores on both of the tests. Even with the evidence that he did know how much he should study, we still have a hard time believing that we don't always have to tell him what to do. Commanding is a big communication block for us.

We're trying to understand that kids need to struggle to make their own decisions. My wife points out that I keep telling our son what to do, and she does as well. Learning how to trust the process of growth and support our son is so foreign to us.

We are continuing to work with Cynthia so that we can make deep changes in our belief structure because we want our son to trust us and even ask us for advice sometimes. Right now, when we tell him what to do, he rejects our advice.

Deciding who is responsible for solving a problem is essential to problem solving together. When we give advice that's not ours to give, communication shuts down.

We are so appreciative that we have Cynthia as our parenting coach to lead us through these challenges and come out winners in the end.

Mom Turns Arguments with Teen Daughter Into Cooperation

I try to control my 14-year-old daughter so that I can solve her problems and keep her safe. Isn't that what a loving mom is supposed to do? That was how I was raised. I need to change and learn how to listen to and support my daughter because she tells me so. "Mom, you don't listen. You don't understand. You're not supportive."

We get into arguments. Cynthia is coaching me privately on a biweekly basis to learn new skills. I'm learning that when I give advice, command, and interrogate my daughter, she gets upset because my hidden underlying message is that she is not capable of solving her own problems.

No wonder she gets mad and says, "You think I'm stupid!" Instead, when she comes home upset about her friends, I've been coached by Cynthia to realize that this is her problem to solve. What my daughter really needs from me is to listen, support, and help her come up with her own decisions and solutions.

Since I've been coached by Cynthia, my relationship with my daughter has been much better. Cynthia has given me hope that I can become a better mother and listener.

Acknowledgments

Ally Parenting: A Non-Adversarial Approach to Transform Conflict Into Cooperation is the culmination of 22 years' work developing my parenting education philosophy and accompanying strategies. This book is the direct result of teaching over a thousand parenting classes and coaching sessions. I would like to thank each and every parent who has worked with me, in a class and privately. Your questions brought out my answers, and your successful implementation of our solutions demonstrates Ally Parenting and inspires other parents. For years, I was asked by parents, "When are you going to write a book?" So, here it is. This book illustrates your challenges and the changes you made to turn your families' conflicts into cooperation. Thank you for allowing me to take this journey with you.

I am deeply grateful for the parenting concepts I learned in 1994 from **Michael Popkin, PhD,** in his parenting program, Active Parenting Today. Dr. Popkin has graciously supported my use and expansion upon several of his parenting concepts, which are the foundation of Ally Parenting. Michael, I appreciate your generous spirit and enlightened parenting concepts.

Patty Wipfler has taught me about listening to emotions which has created deeper bonds in my own life and has become an integral part of my work with parents. Patty, you are truly a gifted parenting educator. Thank you for inviting me into the Hand in Hand parenting education family.

Barbara Whiteside of Whiteside Workshops has labeled the communication block me-tooism which is a profound block in my life and in many of my clients' lives. Thank you for letting me share your wisdom.

The Ally Parenting approach wouldn't exist if I weren't a parent with a supportive husband, a determined daughter, and a vision of a respectful and supportive family. **My husband, Bill**, believes in my approach 100%, so he creates parenting concept cartoons, drives me to my speaking presentations, and speaks to his clients and my class attendees about Ally Parenting concepts. Thank you, Bill, for always being my champion and believing that my parenting message will create greater harmony in the world.

To my daughter, Jen, thank you for inspiring me to be a better parent by giving me many opportunities to grow. I also appreciate your willingness to share some of our personal journey together in this book so that we can help other families build the connected and loving relationship we enjoy every day.

My Business Success Team has been invaluable as they gave me weekly input and feedback throughout the process of writing this book. Thank you to my fellow team members, **Pat Dwyer, Marina Rose, Jenna Teague,** and **Susan Tollefson**, for constantly reminding me how important it was to complete my book. As editor, **Jenna** also made my words flow beautifully. Thank you so much, Jenna.

Kimberly Stinson Serrano did the final proofreading for the overall continuity and clarity of this book. She made sure I published a book that I am proud of.

Stephanie Agnew and **Karen Friedland-Brown** of Parents Place have fostered my expertise as a parenting educator for many years. They gave me wonderful opportunities to develop and teach my parenting concepts, both at Parents Place and in the community.

Just as important are my friends who encouraged me to keep going by reminding me how essential my work has been for families. Thank you to **Denise Cannaday, Michele Fleury-DiFranco, Humberto Gomez, Donna Huhem, Ida Jones, Kyoko Lok, Lindsay Pettit, Terri Plemons,** and **Melinda Rudio.** A special thank you to **Daisaku Ikeda** for being my spiritual mentor for 41 years. I couldn't have completed this book without all of your support, love, and guidance. Thank you.

Finally, I appreciate the support and encouragement I have received from the women in the **Polka Dot Powerhouse networking group**, the **Nonfiction Authors Association**, and my **Jazzercise class.** I know that a book is a group effort and because of my group, *Ally Parenting: A Non-Adversarial Approach to Transform Conflict Into Cooperation* was finally born.

About the Author

In **Ally Parenting: A Non-Adversarial Approach to Transform Conflict Into Cooperation**, **Cynthia Klein** offers practical parenting wisdom and strategies and humorously shares her own experience of raising a daughter. Through Cynthia's approach, parents are inspired to look within and develop their inner wisdom about how to rear their children. The success of Ally Parenting is based on parents realizing that the power to transform any conflict into cooperation begins with changing themselves first, and then their children will follow.

Cynthia Klein is a University of California at Berkeley psychology graduate, author, and public speaker. Cynthia has been working with parents of children ages 5 to 25 as a parenting coach and educator since 1994. Cynthia coaches parents privately and designs and presents parenting education workshops for organizations, schools, and businesses. Over the past 22 years, Cynthia has taught more than a thousand parenting classes and private coaching sessions. Cynthia also authored the "Middle School Mom" column for *Parenting on the Peninsula* magazine from 2010 through 2016. If you would like to contact Cynthia to share how you've used Ally Parenting concepts, visit her website, **www.allyparenting.com.** To learn more about working with Cynthia as a parenting coach, educator, or public speaker, please visit her website, **www.bridges2understanding.com.**

CPSIA information can be obtained
at www.ICGtesting.com
Printed in the USA
LVHW040511141020
668668LV00003B/188